# PORSCHE 944

## BRIAN LONG

**VELOCE PUBLISHING**
THE PUBLISHER OF FINE AUTOMOTIVE BOOKS

## Also from Veloce Publishing:

**Essential Buyer's Guide Series**
Alfa Romeo Alfasud – All saloon models from 1971 to 1983 & Sprint models from 1976 to 1989 (Metcalfe)
Alfa Romeo Giulia GT Coupé (Booker)
Alfa Romeo Giulia Spider (Booker)
Audi TT (Davies)
Austin Seven (Barker)
Big Healeys (Trummel)
BMW E21 3 Series (1975-1983) (Cook & Wylie)
BMW E30 3 Series (1981 to 1994) (Hosier)
Citroën 2CV (Paxton)
Citroën ID & DS (Heilig)
Cobra Replicas (Ayre)
Corvette C2 Sting Ray 1963-1967 (Falconer)
Fiat 500 & 600 (Bobbitt)
Ford Capri (Paxton)
Ford Escort Mk1 & Mk2 (Williamson)
Ford Model T – All models 1909 to 1927 (Barker)
Ford Mustang – First Generation 1964 to 1973 (Cook)
Ford Mustang – Fifth generation/S197 (Cook)
Ford RS Cosworth Sierra & Escort (Williamson)
Hillman Imp – All models of the Hillman Imp, Sunbeam Stiletto, Singer Chamois, Hillman Husky & Commer Imp 1963 to 1976 (Morgan)
Jaguar E-Type 3.8 & 4.2-litre (Crespin)
Jaguar E-type V12 5.3-litre (Crespin)
Jaguar Mark 1 & 2 (All models including Daimler 2.5-litre V8) 1955 to 1969 (Thorley)
Jaguar S-Type – 1999 to 2007 (Thorley)
Jaguar X-Type – 2001 to 2009 (Thorley)
Jaguar XJ-S (Crespin)
Jaguar XJ6, XJ8 & XJR (Thorley)
Jaguar XK 120, 140 & 150 (Thorley)
Jaguar XK8 & XKR (1996-2005) (Thorley)
Jaguar/Daimler XJ 1994-2003 (Crespin)
Jaguar/Daimler XJ40 (Crespin)
Jaguar/Daimler XJ6, XJ12 & Sovereign (Crespin)
Land Rover Series I, II & IIA (Thurman)
Land Rover Series III (Thurman)
Lotus Seven replicas & Caterham 7: 1973-2013 (Hawkins)
Mazda MX-5 Miata (Mk1 1989-97 & Mk2 98-2001) (Crook)
Mazda RX-8 All models 2003 to 2012 (Parish)
Mercedes Benz Pagoda 230SL, 250SL & 280SL roadsters & coupès (Bass)
Mercedes-Benz 190 All 190 models (W201 series) 1982 to 1993 (Parish)
Mercedes-Benz 280-560SL & SLC (Bass)
Mercedes-Benz SL R129 Series (Parish)
Mercedes-Benz W123 All models 1976 to 1986 (Parish)
Mercedes-Benz W124 – All models 1984-1997 (Zoporowski)
MG Midget & A-H Sprite (Horler)
MG TD, TF & TF1500 (Jones)
MGA 1955-1962 (Crosier)
MGB & MGB GT (Williams)
MGF & MG TF (Hawkins)
Mini (Paxton)
Morris Minor & 1000 (Newell)
New Mini (Collins)
Peugeot 205 GTI (Blackburn)
Porsche 911 (964) (Streather)
Porsche 911 (993) (Streather)
Porsche 911 (996) (Streather)
Porsche 911 (997) Model years 2004 to 2009 (Streather)
Porsche 911 (997) Second generation models 2009 to 2012 (Streather)
Porsche 911 Carrera 3.2 (Streather)
Porsche 911 SC (Streather)
Porsche 924 – All models 1976 to 1988 (Hodgkins)
Porsche 928 (Hemmings)
Porsche 930 Turbo & 911 (930) Turbo (Streather)
Porsche 944 (Higgins)
Porsche 986 Boxster (Streather)
Porsche 987 Boxster & Cayman (Streather)
Rolls-Royce Silver Shadow & Bentley T-Series (Bobbitt)
Subaru Impreza (Hobbs)
Sunbeam Alpine (Barker)
Triumph Herald & Vitesse (Davies)
Triumph Spitfire & GT6 (Baugues)
Triumph Stag (Mort)
Triumph TR6 (Williams)
Triumph TR7 & TR8 (Williams)
Volvo 700/900 Series (Beavis)
VW Beetle (Cservenka & Copping)
VW Bus (Cservenka & Copping)
VW Golf GTI (Cservenka & Copping)

**Great Cars**
Austin-Healey – A celebration of the fabulous 'Big' Healey (Piggott)
Triumph TR - TR2 to 6: The last of the traditional sports cars (Piggott)

**Biographies**
A Chequered Life – Graham Warner and the Chequered Flag (Hesletine)
A Life Awheel – The 'auto' biography of W de Forte (Skelton)
Amédée Gordini ... a true racing legend (Smith)
André Lefebvre, and the cars he created at Voisin and Citroën (Beck)
Chris Carter at Large – Stories from a lifetime in motorcycle racing (Carter & Skelton)
Cliff Allison, The Official Biography of – From the Fells to Ferrari (Gauld)
Driven by Desire – The Desiré Wilson Story
First Principles – The Official Biography of Keith Duckworth (Burr)
Inspired to Design – F1 cars, Indycars & racing tyres: the autobiography of Nigel Bennett (Bennett)
Jack Sears, The Official Biography of – Gentleman Jack (Gauld)
John Chatham – 'Mr Big Healey' – The Official Biography (Burr)
The Lee Noble Story (Wilkins)
Mason's Motoring Mayhem – Tony Mason's hectic life in motorsport and television (Mason)
Raymond Mays' Magnificent Obsession (Apps)
Pat Moss Carlsson Story, The – Harnessing Horsepower (Turner)
Tony Robinson – The biography of a race mechanic (Wagstaff)
Virgil Exner – Visioneer: The Official Biography of Virgil M Exner Designer Extraordinaire (Grist)

**General**
1½-litre GP Racing 1961-1965 (Whitelock)
AC Two-litre Saloons & Buckland Sportscars (Archibald)
Alfa Romeo 155/156/147 Competition Touring Cars (Collins)
Alfa Romeo Giulia Coupé GT & GTA (Tipler)
Alfa Romeo Montreal – The dream car that came true (Taylor)
Alfa Romeo Montreal – The Essential Companion (Classic Reprint of 500 copies) (Taylor)
Alfa Tipo 33 (McDonough & Collins)
Alpine & Renault – The Development of the Revolutionary Turbo F1 Car 1968 to 1979 (Smith)
Alpine & Renault – The Sports Prototypes 1963 to 1969 (Smith)
Alpine & Renault – The Sports Prototypes 1973 to 1978 (Smith)
Anatomy of the Classic Mini (Huthert & Ely)
Anatomy of the Works Minis (Moylan)
Armstrong-Siddeley (Smith)
Art Deco and British Car Design (Down)
Autodrome (Collins & Ireland)
Autodrome 2 (Collins & Ireland)
Automotive A-Z, Lane's Dictionary of Automotive Terms (Lane)
Automotive Mascots (Kay & Springate)
Bahamas Speed Weeks, The (O'Neil)
Bentley Continental, Corniche and Azure (Bennett)
Bentley MkVI, Rolls-Royce Silver Wraith, Dawn & Cloud/Bentley R & S-Series (Nutland)
Bluebird CN7 (Stevens)
BMC Competitions Department Secrets (Turner, Chambers & Browning)
BMW 5-Series (Cranswick)
BMW Z-Cars (Taylor)
BMW – The Power of M (Vivian)
British at Indianapolis, The (Wagstaff)
British Cars, The Complete Catalogue of, 1895-1975 (Culshaw & Horrobin)
BRM – A Mechanic's Tale (Salmon)
BRM V16 (Ludvigsen)
Bugatti Type 40 (Price)
Bugatti 46/50 Updated Edition (Price & Arbey)
Bugatti T44 & T49 (Price & Arbey)
Bugatti 57 2nd Edition (Price)
Bugatti Type 57 Grand Prix – A Celebration (Tomlinson)
Carrera Panamericana, La (Tipler)
Car-tastrophes – 80 automotive atrocities from the past 20 years (Honest John, Fowler)
Chrysler 300 – America's Most Powerful Car 2nd Edition (Ackerson)
Chrysler PT Cruiser (Ackerson)
Citroën DS (Bobbitt)
Classic British Car Electrical Systems (Astley)
Cobra – The Real Thing! (Legate)
Competition Car Aerodynamics 3rd Edition (McBeath)
Competition Car Composites A Practical Handbook (Revised 2nd Edition) (McBeath)
Concept Cars, How to illustrate and design (Dewey)
Cortina – Ford's Bestseller (Robson)
Cosworth - The Search for Power (6th edition) (Robson)
Coventry Climax Racing Engines (Hammill)
Daily Mirror 1970 World Cup Rally 40, The (Robson)
Daimler SP250 New Edition (Long)
Datsun Fairlady Roadster to 280ZX – The Z-Car Story (Long)
Dino – The V6 Ferrari (Long)
Dodge Challenger & Plymouth Barracuda (Grist)
Dodge Charger – Enduring Thunder (Ackerson)
Dodge Dynamite! (Grist)
Dorset from the Sea – The Jurassic Coast from Lyme Regis to Old Harry Rocks photographed from its best viewpoint (also Souvenir Edition) (Belasco)
Draw & Paint Cars – How to (Gardiner)
Drive on the Wild Side, A – 20 Extreme Driving Adventures From Around the World (Weaver)
Dune Buggy, Building A – The Essential Manual (Shakespeare)
Dune Buggy Files (Hale)
Dune Buggy Handbook (Hale)
East German Motor Vehicles in Pictures (Suhr/Weinreich)
Fast Ladies – Female Racing Drivers 1888 to 1970 (Bouzanquet)
Fate of the Sleeping Beauties, The (op de Weegh/Hottendorff/op de Weegh)
Ferrari 288 GTO, The Book of the (Sackey)
Ferrari 333 SP (O'Neil)
Fiat & Abarth 124 Spider & Coupé (Tipler)
Fiat & Abarth 500 & 600 – 2nd Edition (Bobbitt)
Fiats, Great Small (Ward)
Ford Cleveland 335-Series V8 engine 1970 to 1982 – The Essential Source Book (Hammill)
Ford F100/F150 Pick-up 1948-1996 (Ackerson)
Ford F150 Pick-up 1997-2005 (Ackerson)
Ford GT – Then, and Now (Streather)
Ford GT40 (Legate)
Ford Midsize Muscle – Fairlane, Torino & Ranchero (Cranswick)
Ford Model Y (Roberts)
Ford Small Block V8 Racing Engines 1962-1970 – The Essential Source Book (Hammill)
Ford Thunderbird From 1954, The Book of the (Long)
Formula 5000 Motor Racing, Back then ... and back now (Lawson)
Forza Minardi! (Vigar)
France: the essential guide for car enthusiasts – 200 things for the car enthusiast to see and do (Parish)
Grand Prix Ferrari – The Years of Enzo Ferrari's Power, 1948-1980 (Pritchard)
Grand Prix Ford – DFV-powered Formula 1 Cars (Robson)
GT – The World's Best GT Cars 1953-73 (Dawson)
Hillclimbing & Sprinting – The Essential Manual (Short & Wilkinson)
Honda NSX (Long)
Inside the Rolls-Royce & Bentley Styling Department – 1971 to 2001 (Hull)
Intermeccanica – The Story of the Prancing Bull (McCredie & Reisner)
Jaguar, The Rise of (Price)
Jaguar XJ 220 – The Inside Story (Moreton)
Jaguar XJ-S, The Book of the (Long)
Jeep CJ (Ackerson)
Jeep Wrangler (Ackerson)
The Jowett Jupiter - The car that leaped to fame (Nankivell)
Karmann-Ghia Coupé & Convertible (Bobbitt)
Kris Meeke – Intercontinental Rally Challenge Champion (McBride)
Lamborghini Miura Bible, The (Sackey)
Lamborghini Urraco, The Book of the (Landsem)
Lambretta Bible, The (Davies)
Lancia 037 (Collins)
Lancia Delta HF Integrale (Blaettel & Wagner)
Land Rover Series III Reborn (Porter)
Land Rover, The Half-ton Military (Cook)
Lea-Francis Story, The (Price)
Le Mans Panoramic (Ireland)
Lexus Story, The (Long)
Little book of microcars, the (Quellin)
Little book of smart, the – New Edition (Jackson)
Lola – The Illustrated History (1957-1977) (Starkey)
Lola – All the Sports Racing & Single-seater Racing Cars 1978-1997 (Starkey)
Lola T70 – The Racing History & Individual Chassis Record – 4th Edition (Starkey)
Lotus 18 Colin Chapman's U-turn (Whitelock)
Lotus 49 (Oliver)
Marketingmobiles, The Wonderful Wacky World of (Hale)
Maserati 250F In Focus (Pritchard)
Mazda MX-5/Miata 1.6 Enthusiast's Workshop Manual (Grainger & Shoemark)
Mazda MX-5/Miata 1.8 Enthusiast's Workshop Manual (Grainger & Shoemark)
Mazda MX-5 Miata, The book of the – The 'Mk1' NA-series 1988 to 1997 (Long)
Mazda MX-5 Miata Roadster (Long)
Mazda Rotary-engined Cars (Cranswick)
Maximum Mini (Booij)
Meet the English (Bowie)
Mercedes-Benz SL – R230 series 2001 to 2011 (Long)
Mercedes-Benz SL – W113-series 1963-1971 (Long)
Mercedes-Benz SL & SLC – 107-series 1971-1989 (Long)
Mercedes-Benz SLK – R170 series 1996-2004 (Long)
Mercedes-Benz SLK – R171 series 2004-2011 (Long)
Mercedes-Benz W123-series – All models 1976 to 1986 (Long)
Mercedes G-Wagen (Long)
MGA (Price Williams)
MGB & MGB GT– Expert Guide (Auto-doc Series) (Williams)
MGB Electrical Systems Updated & Revised Edition (Astley)
Micro Caravans (Jenkinson)
Micro Trucks (Mort)
Microcars at Large! (Quellin)
Mini Cooper – The Real Thing! (Tipler)
Mini Minor to Asia Minor (West)
Mitsubishi Lancer Evo, The Road Car & WRC Story (Long)
Montlhéry, The Story of the Paris Autodrome (Boddy)
Morgan Maverick (Lawrence)
Morgan 3 Wheeler – back to the future!, The (Dron)
Morris Minor, 60 Years on the Road (Newell)
Moto Guzzi Sport & Le Mans Bible, The (Falloon)
Motor Movies – The Posters! (Veysey)
Motor Racing – Reflections of a Lost Era (Carter)
Motor Racing – The Pursuit of Victory 1930-1962 (Carter)
Motor Racing – The Pursuit of Victory 1963-1972 (Wyatt/Sears)
Motor Racing Heroes – The Stories of 100 Greats (Newman)
Motorhomes, The Illustrated History (Jenkinson)
Motorsport In colour, 1950s (Wainwright)
MV Agusta Fours, The book of the classic (Falloon)
N.A.R.T. – A concise history of the North American Racing Team 1957 to 1983 (O'Neil)
Nissan 300ZX & 350Z – The Z-Car Story (Long)
Nissan GT-R Supercar: Born to race (Gorodji)
Northeast American Sports Car Races 1950-1959 (O'Neil)
Nothing Runs – Misadventures in the Classic, Collectable & Exotic Car Biz (Slutsky)
Peking to Paris 2007 (Young)
Pontiac Firebird – New 3rd Edition (Cranswick)
Porsche Boxster (Long)
Porsche 356 (2nd Edition) (Long)
Porsche 908 (Födisch, Neßhöver, Roßbach, Schwarz & Roßbach)
Porsche 911 Carrera – The Last of the Evolution (Corlett)
Porsche 911R, RS & RSR, 4th Edition (Starkey)
Porsche 911, The Book of the (Long)
Porsche 911 – The Definitive History 2004-2012 (Long)
Porsche – The Racing 914s (Smith)
Porsche 911SC 'Super Carrera' – The Essential Companion (Streather)
Porsche 914 & 914-6: The Definitive History of the Road & Competition Cars (Long)
Porsche 924 (Long)
The Porsche 924 Carreras – evolution to excellence (Smith)
Porsche 928 (Long)
Porsche 944 (Long)
Porsche 964, 993 & 996 Data Plate Code Breaker (Streather)
Porsche 993 'King Of Porsche' – The Essential Companion (Streather)
Porsche 996 'Supreme Porsche' – The Essential Companion (Streather)
Porsche 997 2004-2012 – Porsche Excellence (Streather)
Porsche Racing Cars – 1953 to 1975 (Long)
Porsche Racing Cars – 1976 to 2005 (Long)
Porsche – The Rally Story (Meredith)
Porsche: Three Generations of Genius (Meredith)
Preston Tucker & Others (Linde)
RAC Rally Action! (Gardiner)
RACING COLOURS – MOTOR RACING COMPOSITIONS 1908-2009 (Newman)
Rallye Sport Fords: The Inside Story (Moreton)
Renewable Energy Home Handbook, The (Porter)
Roads with a View – England's greatest views and how to find them by road (Corfield)
Rolls-Royce Silver Shadow/Bentley T Series Corniche & Camargue – Revised & Enlarged Edition (Bobbitt)
Rolls-Royce Silver Spirit, Silver Spur & Bentley Mulsanne 2nd Edition (Bobbitt)
Rootes Cars of the 50s, 60s & 70s – Hillman, Humber, Singer, Sunbeam & Talbot (Rowe)
Rover P4 (Bobbitt)
Runways & Racers (O'Neil)
Russian Motor Vehicles – Soviet Limousines 1930-2003 (Kelly)
Russian Motor Vehicles – The Czarist Period 1784 to 1917 (Kelly)
RX-7 – Mazda's Rotary Engine Sportscar (Updated & Revised New Edition) (Long)
SCOOTER MANIA! – Recollections of the Isle of Man International Scooter Rally (Jackson)
Singer Story: Cars, Commercial Vehicles, Bicycles & Motorcycle (Atkinson)
Sleeping Beauties USA – abandoned classic cars & trucks (Marek)
SM – Citroën's Maserati-engined Supercar (Long & Claverol)
Standard Motor Company, The Book of the (Robson)
Steve Hole's Kit Car Cornucopia – Cars, Companies, Stories, Facts & Figures: the UK's kit car scene since 1949 (Hole)
Subaru Impreza: The Road Car And WRC Story (Long)
Supercar, How to Build your own (Thompson)
Tales from the Toolbox (Oliver)
Tatra – The Legacy of Hans Ledwinka, Updated & Enlarged Collector's Edition of 1500 copies (Margolius & Henry)
Taxi! The Story of the 'London' Taxicab (Bobbitt)
To Boldly Go – twenty six vehicle designs that dared to be different (Hull)
Toleman Story, The (Hilton)
Toyota Celica & Supra, The Book of Toyota's Sports Coupés (Long)
Toyota MR2 Coupés & Spyders (Long)
Triumph TR6 (Kimberley)
Two Summers – The Mercedes-Benz W196R Racing Car (Ackerson)
TWR Story, The – Group A (Hughes & Scott)
Unraced (Collins)
Volkswagen Bus Book, The (Bobbitt)
Volkswagen Bus or Van to Camper, How to Convert (Porter)
Volkswagens of the World (Glen)
VW Beetle Cabriolet – The full story of the convertible Beetle (Bobbitt)
VW Beetle – The Car of the 20th Century (Copping)
VW Bus – 40 Years of Splitties, Bays & Wedges (Copping)
VW Bus Book, The (Bobbitt)
VW Golf: Five Generations of Fun (Copping & Cservenka)
VW – The Air-cooled Era (Copping)
VW T5 Camper Conversion Manual (Porter)
VW Campers (Copping)
Volkswagen Type 3, The book of the – Concept, Design, International Production Models & Development (Glen)
You & Your Jaguar XK8/XKR – Buying, Enjoying, Maintaining, Modifying – New Edition (Thorley)
Which Oil? – Choosing the right oils & greases for your antique, vintage, veteran, classic or collector car (Michell)
Works Minis, The Last (Purves & Brenchley)
Works Rally Mechanic (Moylan)

# www.veloce.co.uk

First published in 2001 by Veloce Publishing Limited, Veloce House, Parkway Farm Business Park, Middle Farm Way, Poundbury, Dorchester, Dorset, DT1 3AR, England.
Fax 01305 250479/e-mail info@veloce.co.uk/web www.veloce.co.uk or www.velocebooks.com.
Second edition printed May 2016. This edition February 2017. ISBN: 978-1-787111-35-6 UPC: 6-36847-01135-2
© Brian Long and Veloce Publishing 2001, 2016 and 2017. All rights reserved. With the exception of quoting brief passages for the purpose of review, no part of this publication may be recorded, reproduced or transmitted by any means, including photocopying, without the written permission of Veloce Publishing Ltd. Throughout this book logos, model names and designations, etc, have been used for the purposes of identification, illustration and decoration. Such names are the property of the trademark holder as this is not an official publication.
Readers with ideas for automotive books, or books on other transport or related hobby subjects, are invited to write to the editorial director of Veloce Publishing at the above address.
British Library Cataloguing in Publication Data – A catalogue record for this book is available from the British Library.
Typesetting, design and page make-up all by Veloce Publishing Ltd on Apple Mac. Printed and bound by CPI Group (UK) Ltd, Croydon, CR0 4YY.

# CONTENTS

Introduction
& Acknowledgements ......... 4

**Chapter 1 The Porsche story** ............................... 5
The legendary 356 .................. 6
Competition exploits ............. 12
356 developments ................ 14
The 911 and 912 ................... 14
A competition update ........... 16
VW's links with Porsche ....... 17
A joint project ...................... 17
A turning point .................... 18
Progress of the 914 .............. 19
Corporate matters ................ 20
Porsche in competition ......... 22
914 developments ................ 23

**Chapter 2 The 924** ............. 24
End of the 914 ..................... 24
The 924 ............................... 25
The contempoary 911s and the 928 ....................... 27
924 developments ................ 29
The 924 Turbo ..................... 30
The Carrera GT .................... 31
Lessons learnt at Le Mans ......................... 34

**Chapter 3 Birth of the 944** ................................ 40
The 944 ............................... 41
The 944 reaches the market ............................. 52
The 944 in the UK ................ 57
The new car in America ........ 63

**Chapter 4 The early production models** ............................ 67
The 1983 model year ............ 67
The 1984 model year ............ 73
US update ............................ 75
A return to F1 ...................... 77
The 944 for 1985 .................. 77

**Chapter 5 Arrival of the Turbo** ............................... 88
The 944 Turbo ..................... 88
Early press reaction ............. 96
The Turbo in America ......... 101

944 update ......................... 104
The fate of the 924 ............. 109
The Turbo Cup ................... 111
The 944S ........................... 114
Some thoughts on the 944S ............................... 118
Other 1987 model year news ............................... 121
Boardroom drama ............. 125
The 1988 model year ......... 127
Special Turbo models ........ 135
Demise of the 924 ............. 141
Racing in America ............. 141

**Chapter 6 The twilight years** ............................. 144
The 1989 model year in detail ............................. 144
The American market ........ 154
The S2 in Britain ............... 157
A Cabriolet at last ............. 159
The 1990 model year ......... 168
American update ............... 172
Branitzski makes his exit ................................ 173
The Turbo Cabriolet .......... 174
Other 1991 model year news ............................... 174
Another F1 project ............ 179
US review .......................... 179
End of the line - the 968 ................................. 181

**Appendix I Buying and restoration** ................ 184
Body .................................. 184
Exterior trim ..................... 184
Engine ............................... 185
Transmission .................... 186
Suspension, steering & braking system ........... 186
Interior ............................. 186
Spares today ..................... 187
The best buy? ................... 187

**Appendix II Production details** ........................... 188

**Index** ............................. 191

## INTRODUCTION & ACKNOWLEDGEMENTS

The 944 was introduced to fill the gap between the other two front-engined, water-cooled models in the Porsche catalogue - the 924 and 928. Introduced in time for the 1982 model year, at first glance, the new vehicle looked similar to the 924, but had the advantage of being powered by a 2.5 litre engine that was pure Porsche.

The 944 quickly became the fastest-selling Porsche of all time, and in 1985 a turbocharged model joined the range; a little while later, the 944 line-up was augmented by the 16v 944S. Major changes occurred in 1988 following the demise of the 924S, with a complete reshuffle for the 944 range which got bigger engines and more power.

After a lengthy gestation period, a soft-top 944 eventually found its way into Porsche showrooms, and gradually the standard 944 was phased out, leaving only the Turbo and the S2 in coupé and convertible forms. Ultimately, production of the 944 series ended in mid-1991, and the 968 took it's place.

This book follows the development of the 944 from drawing board to replacement in summer 1991, along the way looking at both European and North American markets. It is the full story of this highly-respected machine from Stuttgart.

---

As always, the factory in Stuttgart has been extremely helpful in supplying information and photographic material. As with the other Veloce Porsche titles written by the author, the vast majority of pictures have been sourced from the works' archives or original brochures.

Of the many people who have helped with this project, in particular I would like to thank my friend, Klaus Parr, the archivist at Porsche AG, and his able assistant, Jens Torner. Having visited many archives in the past, I can honestly say that there are very few which can compete; my life would certainly be much easier if all car companies kept their historical records in such good order.

**Brian Long**
**Chiba City, Japan**

# 1
## THE PORSCHE STORY

Professor Ferdinand Porsche had worked for Lohner, Austro-Daimler, Daimler (which soon after became Daimler-Benz) and Steyr, and in Germany had an unrivalled reputation as a designer.

After leaving Steyr, Ferdinand Porsche felt the time had come to establish his own company. Registered in April 1931, a design studio was set up in Stuttgart with a team of hand-picked engineers and designers. This team included Porsche's son, Ferry, who was then just 21 years old.

Ferry Porsche inherited much of his father's natural flair for engineering

*A pre-war catalogue picture for the Porsche-designed Volkswagen, or People's Car.*

*One of the three Type 64 racers built for the proposed Berlin-Rome marathon of 1939. However, the event was cancelled following the outbreak of the Second World War.*

*Right: The Cisitalia drew heavily on an earlier Porsche design - the V16 Auto Union of pre-war days. A very complex piece of machinery, it was powered by a flat-12 engine with a dohc set-up on each bank of cylinders and twin superchargers.*

and, although he wanted to become a racing driver, his father soon put a stop to his aspirations in this direction. This is perhaps fortunate for, without Ferry Porsche, the company, as it exists today, would never have evolved, and neither would the vehicles recognized as the 'true' Porsches.

As Germany's Chancellor, Adolf Hitler was, naturally, very supportive of German industry, and financed the Mercedes-Benz and Auto Union racing programmes to show the world the strength of German engineering. The highly-successful Auto Union V16 Grand Prix car was a Porsche design, of course, but it was the Volkswagen project that provided the basis for the Porsche success story. The Volkswagen was also financed by the Nazi Party - a blessing at the time, but something which caused problems later.

Just as Hitler was approving the final plans for the Volkswagen, the Second World War broke out. During the hostilities, Porsche and his team were moved to the Austrian village of Gmünd, and there they produced many designs, including those for a number of tanks. Because of his 'links' with the Nazi leader, Professor Porsche was arrested and interrogated by the Allied authorities following the war, but was promptly released. After this, he went to Renault and, whilst there, Porsche and his son-in-law were arrested and imprisoned by the French on war criminal charges, with a ransom of one million francs. Ferry Porsche had also been imprisoned for a short time, but his sister had managed to negotiate his release.

However, the Porsche offices in Stuttgart were occupied by the US Army, and Ferry Porsche had little chance of raising the ransom money repairing ex-Army VWs. By an amazing stroke of luck, Porsche was approached by Carlo Abarth (the famous engine tuner) and Piero Dusio, a rich Italian industrialist who, among other things, wanted to build a Grand Prix car.

The Cisitalia, as it was known, drew heavily on the pre-war Auto Union designs, and was very complex. The project was destined to fail, sadly, as escalating costs put a potentially successful car out of the reach of even Dusio's wealth. Nonetheless, it did provide Ferry Porsche with enough money to free his father.

The professor was allowed back to Austria in August 1947, but died less than four years later. His health had never been the same following his imprisonment, but at least he was able to see his son develop a new car bearing the family name.

## The legendary 356

Design work on the Type 356 sports car had begun in Gmünd after Ferry Porsche decided that his small company should construct a vehicle based on Volkswagen components (fortunately, the British had managed to revive the VW factory after the war). The first drawing was dated 17 July 1947, just one month after the project was instigated.

The first chassis was completed in March 1948 and fitted with a prototype open body two months later. The spaceframe chassis on Number One was well designed, but unsuitable for cost-effective series production as it was very labour-intensive to build.

The engine was a tuned 1131cc Volkswagen unit, mounted back to front to give good weight distribution. Unfortunately, it took up too much space to allow for any more than two seats. A number of other problems were encountered with this set-up and, from the second car onwards, the engine was mounted in traditional Volkswagen fashion on a sheet steel platform chassis.

Number One was taken to the European Grand Prix in Switzerland to allow journalists to try the car, and it was at this meeting that Porsche met Rupprecht von Senger, who was particularly enthusiastic about it. Von Senger and his partner agreed to buy the next four cars, and also proved very helpful in getting supplies from Wolfsburg to Gmünd.

The second car was a coupé,

*Porsche Number One pictured in Gmünd in 1948, with Rudolf Ruhrl (Hans Stuck's old race mechanic) at the wheel.*

*The key staff at Gmünd (from left to right): Karl Rabe, Erwin Komenda and Ferry Porsche. Note the 356 model in the foreground.*

completed in August 1948. Aerodynamics were very good and, combined with the lack of openings at the front and the seamless construction of the body, meant that the Porsche was capable of some very high speeds for such a small-engined car.

Announced during the summer of 1948, the car's public debut was scheduled for the Geneva Show in 1949. It wasn't long before a 1086cc capacity was chosen, allowing the cars to compete in the 1100cc Class at international level. In the meantime, in mid-September 1948, Porsche sealed a deal with Volkswagen securing the supply of parts (VW was now back in German hands, headed by the capable Heinz Nordhoff), as well as the use of the Volkswagen dealer and service network.

The Gmünd cars were completely hand-built, their aluminium bodies beaten into shape, as there simply wasn't the money available to tool up. According to Ferry Porsche, 46 cars were built at Gmünd between June 1948 and March 1951. However, figures vary wildly between sources, with most quoting 50 or 51 vehicles.

Serious production began early in 1950 when the firm moved back to Stuttgart. The Porsche site was still being used by the Americans at the time, so the factory belonging to Porsche's neighbours - the Reutter body works - was used initially. Reutter had already been given the contract to build new steel bodies for Porsche in November 1949, and an area was set aside for the motor manufacturer.

The first steel-bodied Porsche was completed in April 1950. There were a number of subtle differences to the Gmünd alloy cars, but they were indeed subtle. In fact, mild and constant updating was to become a feature of Porsche production through the years, as the company preferred to introduce new models that were evolutions of the outgoing vehicle. Even competition Porsches were largely based on production cars during these early days.

At the 1950 Paris Show, an ailing Ferdinand Porsche held talks with Max Hoffman and others to try and get the 356 into America. By the end of 1950, he was gravely ill, and he died a national hero in January 1951.

In the meantime, in December 1950, a small design and management office was purchased near the Reutter works, and a racing shop was attached with just enough room for two cars and four mechanics. It was at this stage in the proceedings that the company was registered as Dr Ing. h.c. F. Porsche KG.

The Stuttgart concern had a staff of 108 at the time, with planned production of around ten cars per month. In the event, this target was easily doubled, and nearly 300 Porsche 356s were built in the year. The 500th German-built 356 was driven out of the works in March 1951, and just five months later the 1000th 356 left the factory.

By March 1951, 1283cc engines were available, and a 1488cc unit followed in October. Although the 1100 engine continued until the end of 1954, there were fewer sales of the smaller capacity models, especially in America, a market that was already very important to the company.

In September 1952, the 1500 gave a refined 55bhp, while the roller bearing engines giving 70bhp became known as the 1500 Super. Other important revisions carried out during 1952 included dropping the old two-piece windscreen, although the distinct V-shape remained until 1955. Stronger bumpers, now moved further away from the body, were also a feature.

The original Porsche factory was supposed to have been handed back in September 1950 but, due to the alert caused by the Korean War, the American authorities held on to it. With no sign of the old factory being returned, another works was built in 1952, next door to Reutter. By November 1952, the first cars were starting to roll out of Werk II.

From November 1953, a roller bearing version of the 1300 was made available, called the 1300 Super.

*An early 356 coupé in the heat of competition. Many of the earlier cars found their way onto race tracks, or took part in other forms of motorsport, such as rallying and hillclimbing.*

Launched at the Paris Salon, this 60bhp unit was shortlived, remaining in production for only six months; all pushrod roller bearing engines were phased out by the end of 1957.

Dr Ernst Fuhrmann began designing the powerful Carrera engine during 1952. In order to keep down actual size, he devised an ingenious system incorporating no less than nine shafts, fourteen bevel gears and two spur gears to operate the dohc per bank arrangement. The beauty in this system lay in the fact that the engine's overall dimensions were little changed from the standard unit. The first engine was up and running in April 1953 - it was right virtually from the start, and testing took place in the new Porsche 550 at the Nürburgring in August.

A Carrera engine was installed in one of the works Gmünd coupés, and entered for the 1954 Liège-Rome-Liège Rally, held that particular year in August. Ferry Porsche's theory was that if the unit could last through such a tough event, it could safely be put into a production car; the decision to use it was made easier after Herbert Linge and Helmut Polensky won the event outright.

In 1954, the staff was increased to 493, but only 1934 cars were produced - 44 less than in the previous year. However, on 15 March 1954, the 5000th German-built Porsche was produced (two years later the figure reached 10,000) and exports now accounted for 60% of production. Interestingly, VW in Wolfsburg was by now employing over 20,000 people to make an average of 670 cars a day, and in August 1955, the one millionth Beetle was produced.

John von Neumann, Porsche's West Coast distributor, was the inspiration behind the Speedster. The Speedster was exactly what Hoffman needed to boost sales Stateside, selling at $2995 in basic form. Based on the Cabriolet but with minimal equipment, such as a cheap hood, a low and flimsy

*A contemporary colour shot of the 356 cabriolet for the works' calender, pictured here at Mount Palomar in Southern California.*

windscreen, and detachable side-screens instead of wind-up windows, it was introduced into America in September 1954. In all, a total of 4854 Speedsters were produced (both 356 and 356A types together), and it became the darling of the racing set.

At the 1951 Earls Court Show, a Porsche 356 coupé and cabriolet were put on display by Connaught Cars Ltd, the first German cars to be shown in England since the end of the war. Before long, AFN Ltd of Isleworth (the company behind Frazer-Nash) became the agent, with imports starting seriously in 1954. Prices ranged from £1842 to £2378, which was quite expensive when one considers that a Jaguar XK120 cost

*The 356A Carrera Speedster of 1957 vintage.*

*An advertising poster declaring Porsche's excellent results on the 1953 Carrera Panamericana. The ex-works 550 of Jose Herrarte Ariano won the 1600cc Class, with a 356 coming in second.*

around £1600 at this time, and the choice of even cheaper British sports cars was almost endless.

The 356A was introduced at the Frankfurt Show in September 1955. There were subtle body changes and suspension improvements to make the car feel more stable going into corners. The 356s were still being used successfully in rallying, to the extent that the Liège-Rome-Liège event was becoming a Porsche benefit. The racing side of competition was left almost exclusively to the Spyders, although there were Class wins on both the Mille Miglia and Targa Florio.

The 1582cc engine came in 1955, with two versions available; the 1600 and 1600 Super giving 60 and 75bhp respectively. The 1300 and 1300 Super continued unchanged in most markets, but had been dropped in America earlier in the year and were phased out completely by the end of 1957. The 1500GS Carrera engine was made available for the new 356A range and, like the other power units, could be specified in the updated coupé, cabriolet or Speedster bodyshells.

On 1 December 1955, the old works was at last handed back to its rightful owner. Called Werk I, the management, along with the Design, Experimental and Racing Departments, moved there, as well as the Repair Shop. Towards the end of 1955, three out of every four cars produced by Porsche (which by now employed around 600 people) were exported, the majority of which found their way to the shores of America.

There were fewer changes to the cars as production rose; teardrop tail lights replaced the twin round items in March 1957, but by far the biggest changes came when the T-2 body was introduced at the 1957 Frankfurt Show. Following the event, the Carrera became available in two versions - a De Luxe (GS) model with different carburation and an improved heater, and the GT. The 110bhp GT was available only as a Speedster or coupé, and was aimed squarely at competition.

In August 1958, the Speedster was superseded by the Convertible D (the D being added in recognition of the coachbuilder, Drauz of Heilbronn), with a more serviceable hood, a better windscreen, padded seats and wind-up

11

side windows - it was much more in line with Ferry Porsche's ideals.

## Competition exploits

Based on the original Porsche Number One, the Type 550 made its debut in May 1953 for the Eifelrennen at the Nürburgring. On this occasion, the mid-engined car was powered by a 1500 Super unit, but nevertheless narrowly beat the Borgwards to take a maiden Class victory. It provided the Porsche concern with the foundation stone on which to build a racing legend.

By the end of 1954, the first of the customer cars were being completed by Wendler of Reutlingen. The Type 547 Carrera engine was used, but tuned to bring the power up to over 100bhp. The official designation was 550/1500RS, but Max Hoffman coined the name Spyder, and it was this that stuck in the public's mind.

Excellent results at Le Mans, on the Carrera Panamericana, the Mille Miglia (the 1954 event was the international debut of the 550 Spyder with the Carrera engine), the Tour de France Automobile, Tourist Trophy, and numerous tracks across Europe and America secured the Spyder a place in racing history.

The Wendler-bodied 550A had been introduced in April 1956. Gone was the ladder chassis of the old Spyder, replaced by a lighter but stiffer spaceframe, and it incorporated a low pivot swing axle rear suspension. The 550A gave Porsche its first taste of victory on the Targa Florio, and there were many Class wins.

The Type 718 prototype was built up over the winter of 1956/57. Based on the one-off Type 645, it was a lighter machine again, built around a spaceframe chassis and some 125mm (5in) lower than the old 550 Spyder. An improved suspension, superior braking and 142bhp resulted in a far better car. The mid-engined 718 RS became the 718 RSK through further suspension changes; these were later changed back but the RSK name stayed.

Formula Two returned in 1957, the new regulations dictating that 1.5 litre engines running on pump fuel would form the basis for the series. Porsche entered a couple of races, and actually won the F2 Class at the Nürburgring Grand Prix with a 550A.

The RSK had made only two appearances at the race track in the 1957 season, but by the early part of 1958, the definitive 718 RSK had arrived. On the 1959 Targa Florio, Edgar Barth and Wolfgang Seidel claimed Porsche's second victory on the classic event, followed home by three other Porsche drivers.

As early as 1953, Ferry Porsche had hinted that Porsche may become involved in Grand Prix racing. During October 1958, the CSI announced that Formula One would run with 1.5 litre cars with a minimum weight of 500kg for 1961: the rules seemed ideally suited to Porsche. In the meantime, the company continued to field the RSK in Formula Two races. A programme was instigated so that Porsche would have an open-wheeled F2 car for 1959, using it as a test-bed for the proposed F1 machine for 1961. It was running by April 1959, and was very much the same as the Type 718 under the skin, save for the new narrow chassis frame and detail changes that this necessitated.

The car was improved as the season progressed. Stirling Moss was impressed enough by the German car to test it, with the result that Rob Walker was loaned one of the new works F2 cars for Moss to use during the 1960 season. Porsche won the 1960 Formula Two Championship.

The company's F1 debut came at Brussels on 9 April 1961, but it consistently failed to achieve the desired results. Dan Gurney's victory in the 1962 French Grand Prix was to be Porsche's only win in a World Championship event. Formula One proved to be too expensive, and, despite having invested a small fortune in developing the flat-eight engine, Porsche decided to cut its losses and withdraw gracefully from the Grand Prix arena.

To meet the ever-increasing threat from Alfa Romeo and Lotus, Porsche exploited FIA rules to the limit and had a new Carrera prepared to keep its position at the top of the 1600 Class. 25 chassis were reserved by Porsche for the Abarth-Carrera project, although eventually only 20 of the lightweight Zagato-bodied cars were built. Four or five were made ready for works drivers in 1960 - class wins came at Le Mans, on the Targa Florio, at Sebring and the Nürburgring.

The RS60 had a larger windscreen than the old RSK to comply with new FIA regulations for 1960. Otherwise,

*An RS61 coupé. Looking at the styling in profile, it becomes clear that the 904 which followed was a natural piece of evolution. However, unlike the 904, there was also an attractive Spyder version of the RS61.*

*A delightful publicity shot of the 356B coupé, introduced in September 1959. Note the higher mounting of the bumpers and the smoother air intakes, two of the features that help to distinguish the 356B from its immediate predecessors.*

*The 356C signified the end of the line for the classic 356. A new four-cylinder Porsche, the 912, which looked almost identical to the 911, was duly introduced in May 1965.*

the RS60 was basically similar to the 718, except for the slightly longer wheelbase and more powerful engine. The similar-looking RS61 followed for the 1961 season.

## 356 developments

The 356B made its public debut at the 1959 Frankfurt Show, distinguished by the higher position of the headlights in a new wing-line, and higher and stronger bumpers. The standard 1.6 litre 60bhp engine of the 356A was retained, as was the Super, but this was now known as the Super 75 to differentiate it from the new Super 90. This 90bhp unit was available from March 1960, and was considered powerful enough to render the Carrera model unnecessary. For the time being at least a Carrera was not listed.

The 356B was initially catalogued with three body styles: the Convertible D was renamed the Roadster, and the coupé and cabriolet made up the range. In August 1960, these were joined by the shortlived Karmann hardtop coupé. A third factory (Werk III) had been built at Zuffenhausen towards the end of 1959 to cope with the workload, and by 1960 turnover was around 90,000,000 DM a year.

At the Frankfurt Show in September 1961, the T-6 body made its debut. A number of new features distinguished the latest model; the larger front and rear windows on the coupé, a new engine cover with two grilles fitted across the range, and a larger front hood featuring a squarer-shaped leading edge (which in turn led to more luggage space). At the same time as the T-6 356B was introduced, the Carrera returned to the line-up. Named the Carrera 2, it had a two-litre version of the Carrera engine, and was sold to the public from the following April. The Carrera 2 introduced disc brakes to the Porsche marque for the first time, and with 130bhp on tap, a top speed of 124mph was possible. The 50,000th German-built Porsche left the line in April 1962, but shortly afterwards the Karmann hardtop coupé and the Roadster were discontinued due to falling sales.

Introduced in July 1963, the 356C was basically a stopgap model until the new 911 became established. More refined than its predecessors, the body was very much the same as that of the 356B (offered in coupé and cabriolet forms, with the option of a detachable steel hardtop for the latter); the main changes were mechanical. There were new 75 and 95bhp engines, a modified rear suspension, and disc brakes were standard across the range. However, the basic layout of four air-cooled cylinders, horizontally opposed in pairs, remained unchanged throughout the 17 year lifespan of the 356. The body had changed little, but all the time it was being brought up-to-date, regularly acquiring features tested in the field of motorsport.

Porsche thought that a white cabriolet completed in September 1965 was going to be the last 356, and indeed it was officially, but then the Dutch Police placed a special order for ten vehicles in 1966, which were initiated in March. The total number of 356s built came to 76,313.

Despite the demand for the 356, it was obvious that the model wasn't going to last forever, and Porsche started to prepare for its ultimate replacement in the late-fifties. Ferry Porsche wanted the new car to be slightly bigger and a true 2+2. The Type 695 project began in 1959, but was later rejected in favour of a new coupé design from Butzi Porsche - the Type 901.

## The 911 and 912

Butzi (officially Ferdinand Alexander), was the eldest of Ferry Porsche's sons,

*On the left is the Type 901 (which went into production as the 911), while in the centre of the picture is the mid-engined 904 competition car. Ferry Porsche can be seen sitting over the front wheel of this fantastic machine, styled, like the 901/911, by Butzi Porsche, Ferry's son. The photograph was taken during a dealer visit from America in 1963.*

*Porsche stalwart Sobieslav Zasada and his two-litre 911T on the 1968 Monte Carlo Rally. The event was won by Vic Elford in another Stuttgart machine.*

born in 1935. He joined Porsche's Styling Department in 1957, taking charge of it four years later, but this was not a case of providing top jobs for the family; Butzi went on to become a very accomplished designer. Erwin Komenda, who had been with Porsche since its earliest days, did the engineering side of the bodywork.

However, with the flat-four getting close to the end of its development, it was also necessary to look at a new engine. The flat-four was powerful enough in Carrera guise, but these were expensive to build so, in 1961, design work on a new power unit was initiated. As time passed and the Type 901 project came closer to becoming reality, it was decided that the flat-eight Grand Prix engine would form the basis for the new unit. The definitive flat-six Porsche engine appeared in autumn 1963. Overseen by Hans Tomala (former head of the R&D Department) and known as the Type 901, it was a 1991cc, all-alloy, air-cooled unit with a single overhead-camshaft per bank driven by chains. Originally, three single-choke downdraught Solex carburettors were used on each bank, but these were replaced by triple-choke Webers from the beginning of 1966. To overcome oil surge during hard cornering, the 130bhp power unit was given dry sump lubrication.

The Porsche 901, whilst retaining many of the features of its predecessor, was a completely new car. Although the rear-mounted, air-cooled boxer engine layout was kept, along with the famous Porsche baulk-ring gearbox and all-round independent suspension, it was a larger vehicle. The 901 was first seen at the Frankfurt Show in 1963, but the production cars didn't roll off the line at Zuffenhausen until the following year. By that time, the 901 designation was altered to 911 after a complaint from Peugeot regarding the use of "its" numbering system.

The 911 was eventually made

*A 911 Targa from the 1970 model year, by which time the 911's six-cylinder power unit had been bored out to 2.2 litres. Note the now-familiar alloy wheels.*

available to the public at 21,900 DM from September 1964. Then, in May 1965, Porsche introduced the 912. The body, suspension and braking system was identical to that of the six-cylinder 911, but the 912 was far closer to the 356 in that they shared the same Super 90 power unit, albeit in modified form. Most of the 356s built in 1965 had gone to the States, and the 911 was produced alongside the 356 in the latter's final years.

The 911 was introduced to the American public at the start of 1965. The 912 was announced in July 1965, going on sale two months later, just as the 356 series officially ran out. The American market remained the most important for Porsche and its pricing policy there was interesting. In its final year, an SC coupé would have cost $4577 in basic form, whilst the 911 was $6490. The 912, however, was just $4690 - about the same as the earlier four-cylinder model.

Initially, two versions of the 912 were on offer: the 912/4 with a four-speed transmission and the 912/5 with a five-speed 'box. Whereas the 911 had five gauges on the wood-trimmed fascia, the 912 had only three and no wood. Capable of around 115mph, 0-60 came up in a fraction under 12 seconds - performance was therefore about the same as for the 356C 1600SC coupé.

Perhaps the most important change during the early life of the new car was the availability of the Targa body (announced in September 1965 but not sold until the following year), listed for both the 911 and 912. During 1966 and 1967 respectively, two more variations on the 911 were announced - a 160bhp 911S (capable of 140mph) and the basic 911T. At the same time, Porsche's trademark five-spoke alloy wheels were announced and a semi-automatic 'Sportomatic' gearbox became an option.

Not surprisingly, with Porsche's policy of constant evolution, a second generation 911 (the B-series) was launched in September 1968, with a longer wheelbase and flared wheelarches covering the wider wheels and tyres. The 911E was introduced at this time, placed in-between the T and S. While the T retained its twin Weber carburettors, both of the higher-powered machines now featured Bosch mechanical fuel-injection.

In the following year, the engine size grew to 2195cc via an increase in the bore, with power outputs now being quoted at 125, 155 and 180bhp respectively for the T, E and S grades (the latter two models came with fuel-injection and a five-speed gearbox as standard). This 2.2 litre range was subsequently christened the C-series.

Approximately 30,000 911s were built from 1965 to 1969, along with a similar number of 912s over the same period. The 911 was proving itself an excellent rally car, winning the prestigious Monte Carlo Rally in 1968, 1969 and 1970, and for the 1970 season, there was a new four-cylinder Porsche, introduced at the 1969 Frankfurt Show.

## A competition update

Ferry Porsche gave the go-ahead for a new mid-engined competition car at the end of 1962 - the 904. The lightweight glassfibre body (grp was chosen to speed up production, as four or five cars had to be built each day if the new model was to be homologated for the 1964 season) was bonded to the chassis for extra strength. Records show that well over 100 were built, with most of the works cars having six- or eight-cylinder power units.

The new model's first major race was at Sebring in March 1964, where it ran as a prototype - it was eventually homologated in April. Shortly after, the 904 driven by Colin Davis and Antonio Pucci won the 1964 Targa Florio, with Linge and Balzarini finishing second. Ultimately, the 904 dominated two-litre sports car racing during the 1964 and 1965 seasons.

Ferry Porsche had already approved production of another 100 cars, but then Ferdinand Piech (the son of Ferry's sister, who had joined the company in 1963) took over the Research & Development Department and, therefore, the competition shop. Piech had grander ideas and from now on Porsche's philosophy on racing changed quite substantially, with the cars moving further and further away from their road-going counterparts. Piech set

*A 906 (or Carrera 6) on the 1966 Targa Florio. Porsche won the Targa that year, and, indeed, every year thereafter up to and including 1970. The 906 completed the transition from road/race car to pure racer, although the company's motorsport philosophy was destined to change once again in the early 1970s.*

the marque on a route of producing pure racers, culminating in the all-conquering 917.

Among numerous outstanding victories, Porsche won the Targa Florio in 1966, 1967, 1968, 1969 and 1970 (all with different drivers) and again in 1973. However, in September 1971, Ernst Fuhrmann returned to the Porsche camp following a tenure at the Goetze piston ring company and duly took Piech's place as head of engineering.

It's interesting to note, given the close bond between race and road machines in the 356 era, that Fuhrmann considered the current breed of racers too far removed from the road vehicles to be of any real use in marketing. It will be remembered that, not long after his new appointment, a whole range of sporting machinery stemmed from the 911 and, once again, Porsche road and racing cars were unequivocally linked.

### VW's links with Porsche

After signing an agreement in 1948, as well as allowing Porsche access to components and the use of the Volkswagen sales and service network, Nordhoff had provided the Stuttgart firm with a constant stream of commissions. Indeed, Porsche had dealt with around 60 projects for VW before the 914 model was instigated, which ranged from complete cars for the marque to engines and transmissions, and more mundane items such as heating systems.

Early projects - some actually started in Gmünd - included the designs for a complete car that was slightly smaller than the Beetle, and even an electrically-driven machine. One of the most interesting design proposals to come from Porsche was the Type 672 of 1955. This was to be a small car with a rear-mounted, underfloor engine. Tests were carried out with V6s of 1.2 and 1.5 litres, but eventually an air-cooled flat-six was chosen; the 1.5 litre version produced 54bhp, and was without doubt a glimpse of the future.

Another noteworthy Porsche design for VW was the stillborn Type 700, an early form of people carrier. Then, in March 1958, Porsche was commissioned alongside VW's own styling department and Ghia of Italy to design a new bodyshell for a medium-sized car. Porsche came up with several variations powered by an underfloor flat-four engine. The Type 728 (or EA-53 in Volkswagen terminology) eventually resulted in the VW Type 3. Meanwhile, Porsche had developed a number of improvements for the Beetle, including the synchromesh gearbox which was adopted on this most famous of Volkswagens from 1951.

In view of the vast history shared by Porsche and Volkswagen, it was perhaps inevitable that the two companies should at some stage produce a joint project. This happened in the mid-1960s when both concerns were faced with a dilemma.

### A joint project

The Beetle eventually replaced the Model T Ford as the most successful automobile ever made in February 1972, as production easily passed the 15 million mark. But sales had been starting to fall for several years beforehand as competition increased from a new breed of economy cars. New models were in hand to cover this sector of the market, but the Karmann Ghia was also deemed out of date, so a new affordable two-seater sports car was needed.

Porsche was also in need of something new. The price of the 911 had escalated far more than the Stuttgart firm had anticipated, and the cheaper 912 was not selling anywhere near quickly enough to keep the dealers happy, mainly because less-expensive but equally competent sports cars were coming from a number of other manufacturers.

On introduction, the price of a four-speed 912 was $4690 or, put another way, around 72% of the cost of a 911. The body/chassis modifications applied to the 911 series were carried over to the 912, but by 1968 the price of the four-cylinder car was within just 12% of the basic six-cylinder model - it simply wasn't worth Porsche selling it any cheaper. With substantially less power on tap but very little difference in the cost, naturally enough most buyers opted for the 911 and sales were very slow.

Porsche needed an entry-level machine that would sell in volume, preferably using a six-cylinder engine in the interest of standardisation. But developing a new model was a costly undertaking and, besides, Porsche hadn't either the finance or production capacity - a joint project with VW was the obvious answer. Ferry Porsche went on record stating that it came about "from the realization that we needed to broaden our programme at a less costly level and that we couldn't do it alone."

At this early stage, whilst talking over the arrangements, Nordhoff agreed that if Porsche designed and helped develop the new sports car, the Stuttgart company could use the bodies in order to ultimately make two versions - one with a VW engine and badge, and a more powerful model with a Porsche crest on the bonnet and six-cylinder unit. Of course, the cost to Porsche would be significantly less than a body of its own, as VW would be placing orders in much larger quantities. It was the perfect solution for both concerns, as Volkswagen (apart from having Porsche's expert input in a field in which it had little experience) would have a replacement for the Karmann Ghia, and Porsche would gain access to a much-needed high-volume seller without having to invest in expensive tooling and development costs.

Through decades of racing experience, Porsche knew the mid-engined concept was ideal for sports cars, the superior weight distribution aiding handling. It was only a matter of time before Porsche would adopt this layout for a road car, and VW was more than happy to back the proposal. The possibilities of adapting the 904 for road use had been looked into in the past, but the idea was rejected. In any case, the design for the new sports car had to be far more practical and, as part of the brief, had to look neither too much like a Porsche or a Volkswagen, whilst at the same time being agreeable to both parties.

A proposal from Gugelot, a German industrial design concern, was acquired by Porsche in autumn 1966 and duly developed into the 914. The final designs were passed by Volkswagen in 1967. As Karmann was producing the Karmann Ghia at the time and had been heavily involved with both companies in the past, it was a natural choice to build the bodies for the new car. It was agreed that the VW model would be completely built, assembled and trimmed in Osnabruck, whilst the six-cylinder version would be shipped as a plain bodyshell to Zuffenhausen so that Porsche could assemble and finish the machine on the same line as the 911.

## A turning point

Ferry Porsche and Heinz Nordhoff had enjoyed a splendid working relationship for many years, but Nordhoff was due to retire in 1970. In preparation, Kurt Lotz was brought in as Nordhoff's deputy to gradually take over the reins in mid-1967. However, Nordhoff became seriously ill, giving the newcomer no time at all to learn of Nordhoff's personal arrangements with individuals.

On 1 March 1968, the first prototype 914 was driven, but then, on 12 April, Professor Heinz Nordhoff died. Lotz knew nothing of the 'gentleman's agreement' on the supply of 914 bodies from Karmann. Although this wasn't unusual, as the two men often worked on a verbal deal, quite naturally, Lotz wanted to see something in writing. Eventually, after much negotiation, an agreement was reached whereby Porsche and Volkswagen would form a separate company, both partners having a 50% holding. The plan was announced in January 1969, and in the following April, VW-Porsche Vertriebsgesellschaft GmbH (or VG for short) was established in Stuttgart with a working capital of DM 5 million. This new concern would be responsible for the marketing and distribution of the VW-Porsche 914 series and the 911 in most markets with the notable exception of America, which would have its own sales organisation. Although, on the face of it, this seemed a rather dramatic move, it was, in effect, little more than making a previous arrangement official, for everywhere except Britain and France, Porsche cars were distributed through VW outlets anyway. Nonetheless, the

*An early 914/6. Like the 912, apart from a few minute details, outwardly, there were remarkably few features from which to readily distinguish the four- and six-cylinder models.*

announcement sent rumours around the globe about a possible merger until they were quashed by a blunt Stuttgart press release.

In the meantime, Lotz asked Porsche to develop the successor to the Beetle (EA-266), along with Audi and NSU. (Auto Union had been bought by Daimler-Benz over 1958/59, but executive control shifted to Wolfsburg in 1964 and Audi AG was formed. At the end of the decade, Volkswagen - which was then building more than a million cars a year - bought the ailing NSU concern and duly merged it with Audi in summer 1969.) However, after much development work under the supervision of Ferdinand Piech (said to have cost up to DM 250 million), the whole programme was eventually cancelled in the early-1970s as the vehicles would simply have been too costly to produce.

## Progress of the 914

There were to be two different models. The Volkswagen version, the 914/4, would be powered by the 1679cc, air-cooled, flat-four engine from the 411E model using VW's new electronic injection system, allowing it to meet all the American emission requirements (including those for California).

The Porsche model, known as the 914/6, would be equipped with the classic six-cylinder, air-cooled engine from the 1969 model year 911T, rated at 110bhp - 30bhp more than the VW unit installed in the 914/4. As a matter of interest, there were three 911 engine options available at that time: the 911T, the 140bhp 911E and the top-of-the-range 170bhp 911S.

Incidentally, the 1969 model year engine was chosen for the 914/6 as this kept the new model at two litres; the 911 range had been given 2.2 litre engines (available in three states of tune) for 1970, introduced alongside the new 914/4 and 914/6 at the 1969 Frankfurt Show. Initial plans called for a total of 30,000 cars a year, the 1.7 litre, four-cylinder model commencing in October 1969, while 914/6 production was due to start at the end of the year, replacing the 912 in the Porsche range.

Part of the agreement with Volkswagen stipulated that the 914 range would be badged as VW-Porsche. The only exception to this rule was in America, where all models would be Porsches regardless of the powerplant, and sold through the newly-formed Porsche+Audi sales organisation based in New Jersey.

By 1970, Porsche was producing about 70 cars a day, taking the annual total to 16,757. Now capitalised at DM 20 million, the factory employed around 4000 people. However, the 914 was costing Porsche much more than was first anticipated; as a result, the price of the 914/6 wasn't all that different from that of the 911, which reduced its value somewhat in the line-up.

The four-cylinder 914 initially sold for $3695 in America, while the 914/6 cost $6099 (the 911T Targa was $7205 during the same period); due to the high price of the 914/6 and its controversial styling, reactions were mixed.

In the UK, the guide to the 1969 Earls Court Show stated: "History comes full circle with the introduction of cars combining elements of the exotic Porsche and the homely Volkswagen."

It should be noted that Britain had the 914S specification four-cylinder cars only, and the first 914/6 didn't arrive there until May. In UK trim, the £3475 914/6 was capable of covering 0-60mph in 8.8 seconds, before going on to a top speed of 120. No rhd 914s were produced by the factory as the VW element of the partnership was anxious to recoup tooling costs as quickly as possible.

The German price list from November 1970 had the standard 914/4 at DM 11,955, whilst the same model with the popular S-pack option cost just DM 745 more; the standard six-cylinder 914/6 was quoted at a hefty DM 19,980. However, the stronger

*The four-cylinder 914 of 1972 vintage. By this time, production of the Porsche-engined version had been cut back and it was eventually discontinued for the following season.*

economy in Germany led in turn to a weaker dollar, making cars like Porsche's very expensive. The value of the deutschmark had risen steadily against the dollar after the 914 was launched - so not only did it make imported cars more expensive, but if a price was retained in America it also gave less return for the manufacturer in dollar sales.

In fact, by the close of 1970, VW-Porsche's financial results were so bad that it seriously considered abandoning the entire 914 project: after all, a loss of DM 200 million is not something to be taken lightly.

Despite reservations, the decision was taken to continue developing the 914, and a number of detail improvements were duly made. In the meantime, the standard 911 range for 1972 had received another engine size increase, this time to 2341cc, with three power ratings - 130, 165 and 190bhp.

In 1972, the price of the 914/4 stood at $3755. Early that year, the exchange rate was DM 3.2 to the dollar - it had been DM 4.0 in late-1969. A slight price increase in the 914 range therefore meant less profit for VW-Porsche, and the 914/6 subsequently became a special order vehicle in the States. At the same time a 911T Targa was $7985 ($735 more than the coupé), while the top model, the 911S Targa, was priced at $10,230.

## Corporate matters

On 1 March 1972 the Porsche company was reorganized, with all Porsche family effectively withdrawing. Three companies - Dr Ing. h.c. F. Porsche KG in Zuffenhausen, the VW-Porsche VG in Ludwigsburg, and the Porsche Konstruktion KG in Salzburg - came under the control of a holding company, Porsche GmbH, registered in Stuttgart. Ferry Porsche and Louise Piech were the Managing Directors, Ernst Fuhrmann was responsible for engineering and Heinz Branitzki was appointed Finance Director.

The reorganization was completed when Porsche became a joint stock company, Dr Ing. hc. F. Porsche AG. After the family split, Butzi Porsche formed Porsche Design (a highly successful consultancy), and Ferdinand Piech went to VW-Audi, helping to develop Audi's 4wd system which led to the world-beating Audi Quattro. Before too long he was head of the German firm ...

In the meantime, important events were taking place at Volkswagen.

*One of the all-conquering Porsche 917Ks (seen here in John Wyer/Gulf colours) pictured alongside the 914/6. The 914 model also established an impressive competition history.*

*Bjorn Waldegaard (right) and the 914/6 GT that he drove on the 1971 Monte Carlo Rally.*

VW had once again lost money in 1971, and the following year Opel overtook VW as the leading German manufacturer in terms of output. Lotz resigned in September 1971, with Rudolf Leiding taking his place. Leiding was a production specialist and it was obvious that he supported the new direction instigated by the K70. Originally an Audi-NSU prototype, it catapulted VW into the world of fwd water-cooled machines. Introduced as the VW K70 in 1971, it spelt the end of the NSU marque, and one had to wonder about the future of an air-cooled, mid-engined vehicle ...

## Porsche in competition

Porsche had a reputation to uphold. The company had won the Manufacturers' Championship in 1969, and in May that year built 25 examples of the car known as the Type 917.

The model's first victory came in a relatively minor race at Zeltweg towards the end of 1969, but a revised version called the 917K arrived in time for the 1970 Daytona 24-hour Race. There was no looking back as the 917 totally dominated the racing scene for the next four years.

In a bid to promote the 914 series, the decision was taken to develop the machine for competition. The 914/6 GT was homologated in March 1970 and a total of 12 works cars built in the Zuffenhausen Competition Department.

At Le Mans that year, the Porsche marque dominated the legendary 24-hour race to take the first of many overall victories at the Sarthe circuit.

Porsche veteran Hans Herrmann and Britain's Richard Attwood took their Austrian-entered 917K to victory, and were followed home by two other Porsches. The excellent performance of Guy Chasseuil and Claude Ballot-Lena in a 914/6 GT was somewhat overshadowed, but their win in the Grand Touring category was a significant result for the lone 914/6 model, not least because this equated to sixth overall. The Marathon de la Route at the Nürburgring was a 914/6 benefit, and, after a series of other good results, Porsche duly secured the 1970 International GT Trophy by a comfortable margin.

The 914/6 made its official works rally debut on the 1971 Monte Carlo Rally, although a single entry on the 1970 RAC Rally served as a trial run for the most prestigious event on the rallying calendar. Using the same drivers that gave the Stuttgart firm first, second and fourth places on the 1970 Monte - Bjorn Waldegaard, Gerard Larrousse and Ake Andersson - Porsche prepared three new 914/6s for the 1971 event. Waldegaard finished first in Cass with a highly respectable joint third place overall. This was the last works appearance of the 914 in rallying,

although the model managed to claim the 1971 IMSA GTU Championship.

The Porsche 917 took the flag once again at Le Mans, thanks to Helmut Marko and Gijs van Lennep, although the two 914/6s entered fared less well with both retiring. (1971 was the last time the 914 model appeared at the famous Sarthe track.) By the end of the year, the 914/6 GT had once again clocked up a vast number of Class wins in Europe and America.

However, apart from the occasional Class win in minor events and appearances in SCCA events, the 914 series was being seen less and less. The 914 had come 13th overall and second in Class in the 1971 Targa Florio, and in the following year's event took a Class win (ninth overall) courtesy of Schmid and Floridia. Appropriately, in 1973, Porsche won the final running of the Targa Florio, not with one of its all-conquering sports racers, but a works 911 Carrera RS driven by Herbert Muller and Gijs van Lennep.

Porsche failed to contest the 1972 World Championship as the new regulations - which introduced a three-litre engine capacity limit - didn't suit the German firm. Instead, attention was turned towards the Can-Am series, the works cars proudly displaying the Porsche and Audi names side by side on the coachwork. Porsche won the series easily in 1972, and then repeated this success the following year. With the 917 now producing over 1000bhp, Porsche took no less than eight overall victories in the Can-Am series, claiming another well-deserved title in America. However, for 1974, the rules changed again and the Stuttgart marque stayed away.

## 914 developments

Initial sales of the 914/6 had looked promising, but demand quickly tailed off. In the first year, 2657 examples were built - well under expectations of around 6000 sales worldwide. During the second year, it was obvious the six-cylinder machine wasn't going to sell, and production was cut back dramatically for the 1972 model year. Indeed, only 229 cars were constructed.

Plans to introduce a bigger-engined, six-cylinder model at the 1971 Paris Salon were duly shelved, the stillborn 916 remaining nothing more than a series of promising prototypes. The 914/6 didn't appear in the 1973 model year line-up, and total production for the type amounted to just 3318 units.

With no 914/6, a new 100bhp, two-litre, four-cylinder model was introduced to take its place, and to meet ever stricter US emissions regulations there was a new 1.7 litre unit for the American market. Both engines retained the Bosch D-Jetronic fuel-injection and a number of other features from the original unit. There was also a new transmission intended to answer some of the criticism levelled at the old one.

The standard 914-1.7 was $4499 and the two-litre 914S was $5049. At that time a 911T Targa would have cost $8760. The 914S tag was soon dropped - Porsche didn't like the S designation being used - and the official 914-2.0 name was adopted by Porsche+Audi. Nevertheless, it should be noted that the concessionaires in Britain and Australia called the 914-2.0 the 914SC, a title that, strangely, was allowed to continue.

Thanks to the new two-litre 914 and the general improvements made to the range, the 1973 model year was the 914's most successful sales period, with annual production just 10% short of the original target of 30,000 units a year. With most of production going to America, this was no mean feat, as the exchange rate was now less than DM 2.5 to the dollar.

The Volkswagen Type 412 had been introduced for the 1973 model year. It was available as either a two- or four-door saloon, or as an estate car, and initially retained the engine of the 411 (Type 4). The 412 power unit went to 1795cc for 1974 in the heavier four-door and estate models, and it was also used in the Transporter light commercial series. For 1974, the same engine replaced the 1.7 litre lump in the 914 series as well.

When the new generation of 911s with impact bumpers was launched in September 1973, it was noted that engine sizes had increased again, this time to 2.7 litres for the mainstream cars, with three-litre powerplants for the top models. This took them even further away from the 914 series in terms of performance and refinement.

A number of limited editions and specials on the 914 were announced, but sales still fell. In America, the subject of pricing again raised its ugly head. In the July 1974 edition of *Road Test* magazine, it was noted: "The 914 was branded 'overpriced' when it was $2000-$3000 cheaper than it is now, which supposedly elevates it into the outrageously overpriced category and the 911, which costs about twice as much, into the scandalously overpriced bracket."

There was nothing that could be done - after all, exchange rates dictated the price, and the Porsche range was barely in line with them. Fortunately, Helmut Schmidt, as Germany's new Chancellor, would bring a modicum of stability in the future.

# 2
## THE 924

In 1974, Volkswagen had been forced to cut back its workforce, despite the launch of the new Passat/Dasher. Other new generation water-cooled cars like the Golf/Rabbit (and the Audi range) eventually pulled the company out of trouble, but, for a while, there was a serious danger that the business may have had to close its doors completely.

By July 1974, when Karmann Ghia production finally ceased, over 360,000 coupés and more than 80,000 cabriolets had been built. It was replaced by an altogether more modern vehicle - the Giugiaro-styled Scirocco, which entered production at the Karmann works during spring.

As Ferry Porsche stated in his book, *Cars Are My Life*, "This complete change of policy by VW naturally called into question the existence of the joint distribution company, the break-up of which had already been recommended by members of the VW supervisory board. Finally, on 8 May 1974, an agreement to that effect was signed. We acquired VW's stake and moved our sales department into the VG building in Ludwigsburg."

The agreement was retroactive to 1 January 1974, and it brought to an end a very uneasy partnership in which both parties seemed to be pulling in opposite directions. Full control of the 914 shifted to Porsche, although a clause in the agreement ensured that, from the outside, it would seem as though nothing had changed. Interestingly, a number of development contracts were cancelled, although Volkswagen and Porsche did not entirely forsake their long-running alliance.

### End of the 914

Changes to the 914 for 1975 were headed by a different bumper design to meet the latest US regulations, and a modified two-litre engine for the States to satisfy even stricter emissions laws. It retained Bosch fuel-injection and virtually the same specification, but the latest anti-smog equipment drained the power further (now a measly 88bhp, while torque was reduced to 105lbft - figures only just above those quoted for the original 1.7 litre unit).

The 1.8 lump was largely unchanged, but a new exhaust system meant less torque, and in California a catalytic converter and extra anti-pollution equipment was fitted on both engines, making them costlier to produce.

In Germany, the price was held on standard models, but in America the exchange rate and additional costs involved in meeting emission regulations pushed even the basic 914-1.8 to $6300. Add options to this and it became a very expensive car.

The two-litre 914 was priced at $7250 against $10,845 for the 912E - a fuel-injected revamp on the old 912 theme. While the latter could hardly be classed as cheap, it should be borne in mind that the 911S coupé was $13,845 at the time, and the Targa-bodied version was no less than $14,795.

On 10 February 1975, Toni Schmucker, an ex-Ford man, took over from Rudolf Leiding at Volkswagen. Carrying on from where Leiding left off, the 1795cc VW engine was stopped for the 1976 MY in the VW range when the Transporter series (the only model other than the 914 to still use it) went to two litres, using basically the same engine as found in the larger of the two 914s. For this reason, only the 914-2.0 was offered for 1976.

Markets were either shrinking, disappearing, or becoming increasingly difficult to satisfy legally. Because of this, the decision was taken to run production down to an absolute minimum and sell the 914 series only in America for 1976 - it was about the only country where any sort of demand existed, at least at a level where a profit could be seen.

The last cars were completed in Karmann's Osnabruck works during the early part of 1976, with final sales during spring. There was no announcement, the 914 was simply allowed to fade away. Although the 914 wasn't quite the sales success Porsche had hoped for, almost 120,000 were built during the model's six-year production run.

## The 924

After Nordhoff's death, the relationship between Porsche and Volkswagen became increasingly strained. A lot of the problem was political, but, whatever the reason, the two companies slowly but surely drifted apart.

Porsche had a more pressing concern, however, as Dr Fuhrmann predicted the end of the air-cooled engine due to ever-stricter emissions and noise regulations. With the collapse of the VG and the 914 on its last legs, this would have left Porsche with only the 911 to sell, an air-cooled machine with its relatively noisy all-alloy, high-revving engine and exhaust system located in one area at the back of the vehicle - not an ideal scenario for the tighter noise restrictions being introduced, particularly in Germany.

A slower-revving, front-mounted, water-cooled engine started to look attractive, as the water jacket absorbs quite a lot of noise, and the bark of the exhaust could be carried the full length of the car, making it easier to pass fixed-position microphone spot checks. It was also reasoned that a front-mounted engine would allow more space for exhaust emission control devices (the much-publicized US regulations for 1975 and '76 were particularly severe, and those originally proposed for 1978 were, frankly, ridiculous) and, an increasingly important factor, make it easier to comply with Federal forward-impact crash tests.

From 1971 there were plans for a front-engined, water-cooled luxury 2+2 (with a larger cubic capacity to maintain power levels), but it would be some time before it entered production, and the projected price was far too high for the vehicle to provide the company with enough turnover to survive with any degree of comfort. Perceived originally as a replacement for the 911 (it was envisaged the 911 wouldn't last beyond 1980), it was later christened the 928.

Porsche still required a cheaper, entry-level model. As it happened, the Stuttgart company had recently designed and developed a two-litre, water-cooled FR (front engine, rear-wheel drive) sports car for Volkswagen, the commission coming officially in the January of 1972 when the VG was still active. Almost from the moment the 914 was launched, Volkswagen had been considering the details for its more conventional successor, and the EA-425 (or Type 924, as it became in Porsche terminology) was to be it, although badged as an Audi to fit in with the then-current VW-Audi-Porsche marketing arrangements.

Testing began, and by spring 1974, tooling was being purchased in readiness for the new model to be built. However, at the last minute, just as the machine had reached the pre-production stage, the management at Volkswagen cancelled it due to a combination of political wrangling and the energy crisis - the consensus at VW was that it would be too expensive to produce, and the Karmann-built Scirocco was sufficient to cater for the small sports car sector of the market (it was developed alongside the Golf under contract number EA-337).

Porsche was given the opportunity to buy back the EA-425 design to put it into production itself, which it gladly did, even though it cost a reputed DM 160 million. The deal was concluded in January 1975, by which time Volkswagen had already spent DM 180 million in development and initial tooling costs.

The 924 was exactly what Porsche needed in the hard economic times of the 1970s, an age of escalating fuel prices and an unusually strong

*A cutaway drawing of the new Porsche 924.*

deutschmark. Meanwhile, the 911 continued to be updated satisfactorily and, as a result, although the 928 project had been started earlier, it was the 924 that reached the market first. At last, Porsche had the entry-level machine it had originally been trying to secure with the 914.

As Volkswagen had commissioned the new sporting coupé for the Audi line, naturally, a high proportion of the components had been sourced from Wolfsburg. Historically speaking, this was nothing new for the Stuttgart firm, but in its mechanical layout the 924 represented a big departure from traditional Porsche practice.

Jochen Freund was the Project Director, reporting directly to Paul Hensler, who had overall responsibility for the development of the 924. Having joined Porsche in 1958, Hensler became the chief of the Experimental Department after Helmuth Bott was promoted.

Porsche was offered the new five-cylinder, 2144cc, Audi 100 powerplant with a view to possibly making a V10 from it for the 928, but decided to use instead the latest four-cylinder, 1984cc, Audi 100 engine (due for introduction in the 1977 MY, which also found its way into the all-new VW LT commercial vehicle and the AMC Gremlin). After a number of Porsche modifications, the fuel-injected ohc unit developed 125bhp and 121.5lbft of torque in European trim.

Porsche opted for a traditional FR layout, employing a transaxle system (a combined gearbox and rear axle unit) to aid weight distribution and traction. Dr Fuhrmann and his team of engineers had specified the transaxle arrangement for the new 928, so it seemed logical to adopt it on the smaller model as well.

It wasn't a new idea (Grand Prix

cars had used the system extensively during the 1930s and '50s) but, despite its undoubted advantages, it was rare on a road car. Alfa Romeo had just introduced the Alfetta range, which incorporated a transaxle, but after a great deal of research Porsche took a slightly different approach to its Milanese competitors.

The engineers in Stuttgart were not overly happy with the quality of the gearchange in other transaxle-equipped vehicles. Using the Alfa as a perfect example, the gear linkage was long, and propshaft inertia due to the rear-mounted clutch put a lot of stress on the synchromesh. To overcome the problem, Porsche kept the clutch attached to the engine flywheel, with power being taken to the rear-mounted, four-speed transmission via a high-quality slim, and therefore low-mass, 20mm steel bar. This small-diameter bar would normally be too whippy, so the clever part was to run it within an 85mm diameter tube with four strategically-placed, sealed-for-life ball bearings, and then using this tube to connect one Audi fwd bell-housing at the front, bolted to the engine, and another at the rear, attached to the gearbox. This tube effectively kept the engine and gearbox as a single unit, maintaining a perfectly straight driveline, and provided a solid mounting for the gearchange and linkage (which found its way to the transmission through an aperture in the rear bell-housing), as well as a handy support for the exhaust system.

Ultimately, in addition to better gearchange quality, the transaxle arrangement, with just two mountings required at either end, afforded a very rigid structure, good balance (weight distribution was 48% front, 52% rear), excellent traction (thanks to the subtle rearward bias), and enhanced crash protection at both ends - a front impact could be partially absorbed by the tube, while a rear-end shunt could push the bell-housing only a limited amount before it fouled with the body. It was quite literally a stroke of genius.

Front suspension was via MacPherson struts and coil springs (as used on the VW Golf) with stronger lower A-arms coming from the Scirocco. The rear suspension incorporated semi-trailing arms with transverse torsion bars - it was basically the same as the 911's, except that it employed parts sourced from the Volkswagen Super Beetle! The rack-and-pinion steering was also from VW, as was the disc/drum braking set-up.

Clothing this mechanical cocktail was an elegant body designed by Harm Lagaay, although the ultimate responsibility lay with Tony Lapine, Porsche's Chief Designer, who oversaw the project. Lapine was born in Latvia in 1930, and spent 17 years with General Motors, working alongside top stylist Bill Mitchell in the States before being assigned to Opel (part of the GM empire). Whilst in Germany, Porsche offered him a position; after Butzi Porsche left the family fold, Lapine assumed the mantle of head of styling and design.

Although the 924 had been expected to make its debut at the 1975 Frankfurt Show, it failed to appear and was eventually launched in November. Engines were to be built at VW's Salzgitter works, and transmissions produced at Kassel; the body was constructed at the former NSU factory at Neckarsulm, where main assembly took place, albeit under Porsche supervision (it was only a few minutes north of Stuttgart).

The 924 became available on the home market first, early examples filtering into the showrooms during February 1976, with prices starting at DM 23,240. It arrived in the USA a few months later classed as a 1977 model year vehicle, duly replacing the 912E in the line-up. Although it had only 95bhp in Federal guise, at just $9395, it was some $4600 cheaper than a 911S coupé and over $1000 cheaper than the shortlived model it superseded.

*Road & Track* carried out a comparison test between the 924, the two-litre Alfa Romeo Alfetta GT (GTV in Europe) and Datsun's 280Z. Despite qualms over the ride and its rather high price, the well-built Stuttgart machine came out the easy winner. "No doubt this is only the first of many victories for the 924," the magazine said. "Perhaps some day even the Porsche fanatics will come out of their ivory tower and learn to love the 924."

## The contemporary 911s and the 928

The six-cylinder engine of the 911 range was constantly upgraded; from 2.2 litres for 1970, to 2.4 litres for 1972, and 2.7 litres for 1974; the Carrera ultimately came with a three-

Publicity shot of an early 924. Compared with many of its contemporaries, the 924 had a timeless look about it. In America, by far the biggest market for this kind of car, the pure lines of the Datsun Z were being spoilt by the onslaught of Federal regulations, whilst other manufacturers such as Alfa Romeo and Lotus adopted the straight-edge styling that was very much en vogue at the time. However, nowadays, it is very easy to place the cars in a certain period. The Mazda RX-7 had yet to appear, of course (it made its Japanese debut in March 1978), while, of the US makers, vehicles in this category just seemed to lack the elegance and subtlety of the Porsche. Naturally, some of the Italian exotics were more stunning, but so were their prices which, more often than not, were in a different stratosphere.

American advertising from 1977 showing the Turbo Carrera and the mighty 936 racer.

*Another piece of advertising from the States, this time for the rather more attainable 924.*

litre unit. The 911 Turbo appeared at the 1974 Paris Salon, taking the world by storm with its electrifying performance. Not only was this the quickest road car to come from the Stuttgart factory during that period, it was also the most expensive, at nearly twice the price of a 911S coupé. However, despite its hefty price tag and the relentless rise in fuel costs, within 18 months of launch Porsche had already sold twice as many as expected.

For the 1976 model year, the European specification 2687cc units were given more power until the normally-aspirated range was standardized at three-litres for 1978. At the same time, the Turbo became a 3.3 litre unit developing a healthy 300bhp. Meanwhile, the range had been simplified to allow another new car to join the Porsche line-up - the 928.

Introduced in February 1977, the 928 made its public debut at the following month's Geneva Show. It was a member of the same family as the 924, with a front-mounted, water-cooled engine and transaxle to give good weight distribution. The engine, in this instance, however, was a V8 unit of 4.5 litres designed to tempt customers who traditionally bought from Jaguar and Mercedes-Benz. The brainchild of Dr Fuhrmann, it was immediately voted 'Car of the Year'.

The 928, being a luxury Grand Tourer, was not cheap by any standards. In America, its largest market, it cost $28,500 on introduction. This compares to $11,995 for a 924, or $19,500 for a 911SC coupé - only the 911 Turbo was more expensive. The 155mph 928S was added to the range in August 1979, with the engine bored out to give 4.7 litres and 300bhp.

### 924 developments

Although the 924 had been displayed in rhd form at the 1976 Earls Court Show, it wasn't until February 1977 that the car went on sale in the UK, priced at £6999. Cars destined for American shores had been substantially improved by this time. Designated as 1977.5 MY models, the latest 924 featured more power, a different final-drive ratio and a number of other refinements.

Despite certain reservations from

*The addition of a turbocharger brought true Porsche performance to the 924 series. According to factory figures for the 924 Turbo, the 0-60 time was cut to just 7.8 seconds and top speed shot up to 140mph. Just as impressive, fuel consumption was only about 20% up on that of the normally-aspirated car - a small price to pay for the lashings of extra horsepower and torque.*

the motoring press, the car was an instant hit in the States, accounting for over 4500 sales in 1976 and more than 13,500 of the 20,000 Porsches sold in America during the following year.

In the UK, the Lux package was soon put together (available from August 1977) and, in keeping with the Porsche tradition of continual development, for the 1978 model year a Porsche-designed, five-speed gearbox was made available as a cost option in all markets. On 24 April 1978, the 50,000th 924 left the old NSU works.

But the honeymoon period was over. In *Road & Track*, John Dinkel noted: "You might think *R&T* is starting to sound like a broken record, but damn it, we're frustrated. The cause of that frustration? Porsche's 924. On paper it has all the makings of a great GT. In truth, the steering, handling, interior layout, seating, instrumentation and styling are all in the Porsche tradition. And we must admit that evolutionary improvements have alleviated a few of the niggling problems that have plagued the 924 since it was introduced in 1976 (especially a classic case of *freeway hoppus Californium*). This brings us to the reason of our discontent: the engine. The Audi-designed two-litre is noisy, rough and buzzy and, adding injury to insult, gives performance hardly commensurate with a GT of the 924's supposed stature and price - now up to $14,600."

In a bid to endow the 924 with more performance, Porsche tried supercharging the model (the project was allocated the Type 931 designation, with the engine being given the 047 appellation). Sadly, nothing came of it; supercharging was considered decidedly old-hat as the turbo era was now in full swing.

Fortunately, Porsche had something up its sleeve. As Chairman of the Management Committee and Director of Engineering since 1972, Dr Fuhrmann naturally had an important role in both the 924's origins and its future course. In 1976 he promised: "Under our guidance, the 924 will develop like a real Porsche."

## The 924 Turbo

As Fuhrmann had promised, the 924 was continually developed and, in response to demands for more power, in November 1978, three years after the new series first appeared, a 170bhp turbocharged version made its official debut. Overseen by Paul Hensler and designated the Type 931 (or 932 for rhd models), the 924 Turbo helped redefine the modern sports car, combining thoroughbred progress with civility and comfort.

While the five-speed manual transmission was still an option on the normally-aspirated 924, on the Turbo it came as standard, along with a larger diameter clutch (up from 215 to 225mm, and now hydraulically-operated instead of by cable). However, in typically thorough fashion, the gearbox mainshaft was strengthened, as were the differential and driveshafts.

Spring rates were altered, the standard Boge shock absorbers were replaced by Koni units at the front and Bilsteins at the rear, and the anti-roll bars were changed - an increase to 23mm diameter at the front and a slimmer 14mm bar for the back. The semi-trailing arms at the rear were also uprated, as were the wheel hubs and bearings, the latter being sourced from the 911SC. This meant a five-stud wheel fitting, but, due to the different offset compared to the 911, this subsequently led to two new alloy wheel designs being adopted. Braking was now via Porsche ventilated discs all-round, with the floating calipers from the 928.

Changes to the bodywork were intentionally minimal: four apertures to direct air onto the oil cooler in the leading edge of the nose, a NACA duct on the bonnet to dissipate heat from around the turbo, further ventilation in the front airdam to provide additional brake cooling, and a neat polyurethane spoiler mounted on the rear hatch. The spoiler not only increased downforce, but also brought the Turbo's coefficient of drag down from 0.36 (for a standard 924) to 0.34.

Left-hand drive production for the home market began in November 1978 at the rate of about 20 cars a day, with right-hand drive cars coming off the line the following summer. It is interesting to note that, unlike the standard 924 engines, which were completely produced by Volkswagen, the M31 turbocharged units were built up and tested in Porsche's own Zuffenhausen works.

The venerable John Bolster was full of praise for the new model: "The Porsche 924 Turbo is a two-litre car that can out-perform most of the so-called supercars at a fraction of their bills. It is also sufficiently light and responsive to out-corner them with ease, while its wide revolution range and flat torque curve render it a most untiring companion on a journey."

Dr Fuhrmann chose to describe it as "a modest improvement," but, judging by the many rave reviews from around the world, it was anything but a modest improvement - it was a transformation. That great enthusiast, Paul Frere, noted: "I think the new Porsche 924 Turbo will go a long way toward getting the breed accepted as a real Porsche among the traditional diehards."

All US 1980 model year Porsches (including the 911 and 928) came equipped with an oxygen sensor. The Lambda-sond sensor screwed into the exhaust manifold and, in conjunction with the fuel-injection system, constantly varied the air-fuel mix to give the most efficient burn, thus allowing the newly-adopted three-way catalytic converter to do its job of cutting down CO, HC and NOx emmissions. It also enhanced engine response and fuel consumption, the latter by as much as 20%.

A new Audi five-speed transmission was introduced on the 924, with fifth up and to the right and reverse below, like contemporary Alfas. This arrangement received a more favourable reception generally, although I've always rather liked the original dog-leg first layout. Anyway, the availability of this cheaper five-speed unit made it viable as the standard transmission for the normally-aspirated 924 in all markets, augmented by the old three-speed automatic. The 924 Turbo retained the Getrag 'box, as the Audi unit wasn't able to handle the additional torque.

The German magazine, *Auto Motor und Sport*, again voted the 924 the 'Best Sports Car' in the under two litre class for 1980, making it four times in a row the baby Porsche had taken the title. Unfortunately, the cost of 924 motoring was still climbing. With a list price of $15,970 (which soon shot up to $16,770), it was almost twice as much as a Mazda RX-7 GS (listed at $8295) and around $6000 more than a Datsun 280ZX - to add insult to injury, both were faster, quieter and better-equipped.

## The Carrera GT

The 924 Carrera GT model was first shown at the 1979 Frankfurt Show as a 'styling exercise,' but revealed Porsche's obvious intent to enter the 924 in the field of top-class competition. Three different Turbo-based prototypes were built, eventually giving the lines for the GT and the forthcoming 944.

Meanwhile, sure enough, in the early part of 1980 a racing model did appear, and was duly given the legendary Carrera appellation. The glassfibre wing extensions covered enormous Dunlop tyres mounted on 16-inch BBS alloys, and the same lightweight material was also employed for the deep front airdam, bonnet and doors. The side and rear windows were made in plexiglass in a bid to further reduce weight.

Although capacity was kept at 1984cc, the power unit featured a 6.8:1 compression ratio, titanium conrods, a larger turbocharger, an

*One of the three prototypes built for the 1979 Frankfurt Show. Note the bulging wings covering the optional 6J x 16 forged alloy wheels offered for the Turbo, the slightly larger rear spoiler and air intake on the bonnet.*

air-to-air intercooler, a Kugelfischer fuel-injection system and dry sump lubrication. With this specification, it developed a reliable 320bhp at 7000rpm and 282lbft of torque at 4500rpm. These new cars, weighing in at 2068lbs (940kg), were based on the successful SCCA racers, so had a coil-spring rear suspension, while the braking system was borrowed from the 917. In keeping with its purpose - to win at Le Mans - it was given a 26.4 gallon (120 litre) fuel tank. Despite the massive wheelarch bulges, Cd was quoted as just 0.35.

Porsche eventually homologated the two-litre 924 Carrera GT as a Group 4/Group B machine (homologation number 672). However, to qualify, at least 400 examples were needed, so a number of road cars found their way onto the market. Ultimately, a total of 406 were produced.

Compared to the standard 924 Turbo, it was easy to identify the Carrera. At the front there was an air intake on the bonnet, and a deeper front spoiler which merged gently into the wider wings, made in reinforced polyurethane. The rear wheelarches were far bigger, too, with the inner sections larger than standard to allow for racing rubber to be fitted (interestingly, because this model didn't inherit the coil-spring rear suspension of the pure racers, there was a cut-out behind the wheelarch extensions to allow easy access to the torsion bar tube). Around the back, there was a deeper glassfibre bumper, a bigger spoiler and discreet 'Carrera GT' badge. As a result of these bodywork changes, the Cd was just 0.34, with the weight a very reasonable 2594lbs (1179kg).

With a KKK turbocharger, air-to-air intercooler (the latter lurking under the bonnet scoop, and allowing an 8.5:1 compression ratio) and Siemens-Hartig digital ignition (a first for a production car), the two-litre M31/50 engine produced 210bhp at 6000rpm and a healthy 203lbft of torque at 3500rpm. Combined with a strengthened Turbo-spec, five-speed gearbox and a 3.89:1 final-drive ratio, this was enough to endow the vehicle

*Road version of the 924 Carrera GT.*

*The purposeful lines of the Type 937, or 924 Carrera GT road car (the 938 number was allocated to right-hand drive versions). The wheelarch extensions and front spoiler were made in reinforced polyurethane, incidentally. It was available in red, black or silver only, the interiors finished in black velour with contrasting pinstripes*

*The Porsche line-up for the 1981 model year. Clockwise from top left: the 928, 928S, the normally-aspirated 924, the 924 Turbo, the 911SC coupé, 911 Turbo and the 911SC Targa.*

with a 0-60 time of 6.9 seconds (one independent test recorded an amazing 5.8) and a top speed in excess of 150mph. Not only that, Porsche claimed it was the most economical car in the range.

The suspension, a subtly uprated version of the Turbo set-up, rode a fraction lower than standard, reducing the car's overall height by about 13mm. Mel Nichols, a *Motor Trend* regular, described it as "perhaps the best road-going Porsche yet."

## Lessons learnt at Le Mans

The Porsche 936 hadn't won the 24-hour classic since 1977, but, despite the fact that the ageing sports racers were favourites for victory in 1980, Dr Fuhrmann decided to leave the works cars in Stuttgart to concentrate the team's efforts on the 924.

Fuhrmann had always strived to adhere to a policy of having a close relationship between race and road cars, so although some members of the press expressed surprise, it wasn't really that big a shock. Besides, 935s (variations on the 911) had filled the first three spots in 1979, so there was still a good chance that a Porsche would take the flag.

The factory entered three 924 Carrera GT models in the GTP Class for 1980, the 924's debut at the famous Sarthe track. With highly-modified bodywork hiding 320bhp turbocharged engines and five-speed Porsche transmissions, the cars were expected to uphold the company's enviable reputation at Le Mans. The Jurgen Barth/Manfred Schurti car was the best-placed 924, coming sixth overall and third in Class after completing 2678 miles in the alloted time. The Andy Rouse/Tony Dron pairing finished 12th, one place ahead of the machine driven by Derek Bell and Al Holbert.

The 924 Carrera GTS was built as an Evolution model of the GT. Just 59 were constructed (a minimum of 50 were required by the FIA), with 20% more power and around 124lbs, or 56kg, less weight. As a result, top speed was over 155mph, with the factory

*A 924 Carrera GTS prepared for rallying. This example was part of a works effort to return to the WRC scene, and was campaigned by Walter Rohrl during the 1981 season.*

*Final preparation for Le Mans 1981. This picture shows the 924 GTP, actually a prototype for the forthcoming 944, although it would be some time before a turbocharged version reached the marketplace. This vehicle, apart from the engine (which produced 420bhp at 6800rpm - 480 had been seen on the testbed), had similar running gear to the GTR.*

quoting a 0-60 time of 6.2 seconds. (Incidentally, the works launched a shortlived attack on the World Rally Championship with the GTS, but it was withdrawn in the face of mightier competition from cars like the Audi Quattro.)

The 924 Carrera GTR also appeared in 1981, and was a customer racing car built as a result of lessons learnt at Le Mans. Weighing just 2112lbs (960kg) in Group 4 trim, the 375bhp engine was enough to give blistering performance and a 180mph top speed. A total of 17 GTRs were built.

There was the usual varied selection of Porsches at Le Mans in 1981, numbering 18 in all. Of these, three were 924-based machines. Car number 1 was a works-entered 924 GTP driven by Jurgen Barth and 1980 World Rally Champion, Walter Rohrl. Having recorded an average speed of 114mph over the 24 hours, it was eventually placed seventh

*Ferry Porsche (left) in the pits at Le Mans in 1981. Jacky Ickx and Derek Bell won for the Stuttgart marque, incidentally, guiding a Group 6 936 to an easy victory; this was Ickx's record-breaking fifth win at Le Mans.*

*The 924 Carrera GTR of Schurti and Rouse being chased by the GTP model in the 1981 Le Mans 24-hour race.*

overall, and third in the GTP Class behind two Rondeaus. This unique car was powered by a 2479cc version of the four-cylinder engine, the same capacity as the forthcoming 944 road car. However, with a 16-valve head and KKK turbocharger being added to the racer, the similarity ended there. Anyway, it provided the factory with an excellent piece of good PR just a couple of weeks before the new model was launched.

The other works 924 was a two-litre GTR model driven by Schurti and Rouse, but gearbox problems resulted in the car finishing no higher than 11th overall. The third 924 was a privately-entered GTR, which retired due to gearbox trouble.

Without doubt, the 924 had now established itself, a long list of developments since launch helping to improve the model (another batch of refinements was introduced for the 1981 season). By February that year, over 100,000 had been produced, and its various derivatives gave a clue to the latest vehicle to augment the Porsche line-up - the 944.

## 3
### BIRTH OF THE 944

Ernst Fuhrmann, Porsche's Chairman since 1972 and designer of the first Carrera engine, was eventually ousted from office in November 1980. Ferry Porsche later stated he felt Fuhrmann had trouble understanding the market (he did come from an engineering rather than commercial background, after all), but there was a definite underlying clash of personalities.

Peter Schutz became Chairman on 1 January 1981, hand-picked by Ferry Porsche. Born in Berlin in 1930, Schutz had spent most of his life in America before moving to the Deutz concern in 1978 to take up the position of Director of Powertrain R&D.

Whereas in recent years Fuhrmann had almost dismissed the 911, preferring instead to direct company resources towards the 928 and the forthcoming 924 derivatives, Schutz made it his mission to revive the legendary air-cooled model and give it the development it needed to remain competitive. Schutz went on record stating: "So long as there's demand for a certain model, we'll go on making it." It was exactly what Porsche enthusiasts wanted to hear, and there was more good news for Porsche fanatics.

The 924 had suffered at the hands of critics, largely because of its powerplant, which - admittedly - had a tendency to become rather harsh at high revs. It also brought the car's pedigree into question. Journalists

*Peter Schutz pictured with the 944. Although Schutz was determined to revive the 911, he realized the importance of the four-cylinder cars, stating that Porsche's future could be very rocky if their potential wasn't developed sufficiently.*

*As with the 924, overall responsibility for the 944 lay with this man, Paul Hensler (Jochen Freund was again appointed Project Director). This photo of Hensler was taken in 1985.*

were delighted to point out that it was "a truck engine," but in fact the unit used in the VW LT van was quite different in a number of important respects. Nonetheless, the damage was done and it was some time before the 924 was finally accepted into the fold.

Fuhrmann had always planned to develop the 924 into a range of vehicles that offered very different characteristics. The standard car could be bought with either manual or automatic gearbox; supercharging was assessed, and the turbocharged model eventually reached the marketplace. There were 924-based racers, and, indeed, a road car version of the latter - the 924 Carrera GT - was sold, combining blistering performance with a fair amount of exclusivity.

The next stage in the model's development was to introduce a normally-aspirated variant with a larger engine displacement; to silence the critics, the unit would be designed and built by Porsche. Enter the 944.

## The 944

The engineers at Weissach (Porsche's excellent R&D facility some miles to the west of the Zuffenhausen works) considered the 2.2 litre Audi five-cylinder engine when development of the 924 began, but decided it was too long and too heavy for a sports car application. Besides, after modifications were made to the four-cylinder unit, despite the smaller displacement, power output wasn't very different.

Experiments later took place with a 924 fitted with the Douvrin-built 2.7 litre PRV V6 (the result of a joint project instigated in 1971 by Peugeot, Renault and Volvo). De Lorean adopted the later 2849cc version of the unit for its gull-winged sports car, though Porsche's people were not impressed.

However, the main reason for cobbling up this hybrid wasn't to assess the PRV engine, but to see what the V6 configuration was like in the model. After all, with Helmuth Bott guiding Porsche into modular powerplants developed from the 928's V8, it was quite possible to shorten it into a six-cylinder unit.

The problem was the large displacement that this would bring about - 3.4 litres, even if the smaller 4.5 litre production engine was used as a starting point. Expense, difficulties fitting the power unit by the same method as that used on the 924 (from underneath), and a less than frugal thirst for fuel, all combined to eventually scotch the idea.

By the early part of 1981, speculation was rife. In the June issue of that year, *Road & Track* noted: "It is an open secret that someday the Porsche 924's Audi-derived engine will be replaced by one bank of Porsche's 928 engine and will probably start life as a 2.2 litre but with room for expansion. Balance shafts are likely to be used to smooth the effects of the in-line four's secondary imbalance, and a prototype of that engine will be seen in this year's factory-entered 924 at Le Mans." Sure enough, as mentioned in the previous chapter, a 2479cc four powered one of the works entries, but, apart from the cubic capacity and the fact that twin balance shafts were employed, it was hardly a true representation of the forthcoming 944 unit. Anyway, an important point was raised in the article; the 944 four was indeed based on the 928's V8.

By taking this route, development time could be reduced (Porsche already had a vast amount of experience with the 928 in service), and a number of parts and machining processes could be shared, thus cutting production costs. Incorporating technology learnt from the experimental TOP (Thermically Optimized Porsche) engine, a team headed by Gerhard Kirchdorfer began work in earnest in spring 1977.

Although the 928 went into production with a 4.5 litre V8, plans for the original engine proposed a

*By drawing on their experience with the experimental TOP engine, Porsche engineers developed a very efficient unit for the 944, with plenty of power yet frugal fuel consumption and exhaust emissions. It had an alloy head, block and sump to save weight; even the cam cover was an alloy casting.*

five-litre unit. Basically, the normally-aspirated 944 powerplant was half of that prototype V8. The bore and stroke of 100 x 78.9mm was retained, resulting in a displacement of 2479cc - very big for a four, as usually two litres is considered the maximum possible without sacrificing refinement. Like the 928, it featured linerless, etched cylinder bores, and the pistons were ferrous plated. The forged steel crankshaft ran in five main bearings in a two-piece, cast alloy open deck block (lightweight Reynolds 390 aluminium alloy with a high silicon content was used in the block's construction, incidentally), while the single overhead-camshaft operated one inlet and one exhaust valve per cylinder via hydraulic tappets in the aluminium alloy crossflow head. (Interestingly, the combustion chamber design and valve angles were different to those of the V8.) As with the 924 unit, a toothed belt was used to drive the camshaft.

Perhaps the most interesting feature was the use of two belt-driven,

*Although the new engine shared a lot of components and machining processes with the 928's V8, the balance shafts were a unique feature of the 944 unit. They were positioned where the two smaller circular protrusions appear on the timing cover.*

contra-rotating balance shafts - something invented by the forgotten genius, Dr Frederick Lanchester, at the turn of the century, but more recently employed by Mitsubishi for its Sigma engine. Running at twice the crankshaft speed, these guaranteed the engine's smooth operation, despite the rather large capacity for a four-cylinder unit. Attempts were made to work around Mitsubishi's patents on the way the balance shafts are attached, although in the end it was easier from an engineering point of view to pay the Japanese company a royalty.

To test the theory, the engineers in Weissach rigged up a pair of external balance shafts on a 924 lump, making them adjustable in order to find their optimum position. This was an important experiment, as a few millimetres either way made the secondary piston inertia forces appear worse than in an engine without this cunning device. Indeed, the belt on the 2.5 litre GTP racer that Porsche fielded at Le Mans slipped a tooth and made the engine run in a very unrefined manner (although, it must be said, the high torque on the competition car made great demands on the toothed belt). Fortunately, the design otherwise proved extremely reliable, at the cost of a measly 4bhp.

The first prototype was up and running only a year after the project started. By using a great deal of shared technology (ultimately, the 928 and 944 engines would have more than 50 common components), it cost Porsche just £5 million to develop - a small sum by the standards of the day.

This Porsche-designed power plant, designated M44/01 (or M44/03 if an automatic gearbox was specified), was equipped with Bosch's Motronic digital electronic ignition system (which also controlled the Bosch L-Jetronic fuel-injection), an electric fuel pump being used to get the petrol from the 14.5 gallon (66 litre) tank. A relatively high compression ratio of 10.6:1 in Europe meant a definite requirement for high octane fuel.

The water-cooled unit, which developed 163bhp and 151lbft of torque in the European spec 944, was canted over 30 degrees to the right to keep the bonnet line as low as possible. The radiator was a sealed unit, employing a separate plastic header tank, whilst a thermostatically-controlled electric fan reduced noise and a needless drain on engine power; the alternator was rated at 90 amps.

Although the 944 engine (which featured an oil-to-water heat exchanger for both quicker lubricant warm-up and enchanced temperature control), was significantly longer than that of the 924, the extensive use of alloys helped keep weight down. In fact, at 339lbs (154kg), the 944's four was just 40lbs (18kg) heavier - a small price to pay for a 31% increase in horsepower and 21% increase in torque over the normally-aspirated 924 powerplant. The size of the unit in relation to its modest cubic capacity was actually quite advantageous, as it would enable a series of bore increases in the future. Indeed, Helmuth Bott, Porsche's head of R&D and later Technical Director, said at the time of the launch: "There is still considerable development potential in this engine. Its capacity can be varied from two- to about three-litres, and we are already working on a turbocharged version."

Special fluid-filled engine mounts were used. The engine sat on a crossmember cast in lightweight aluminium alloy (the steering rack was also bolted to this casting, not found on the 924, with extra rubber bushes added in a bid to reduce NVH), which was then attached to the bodyshell by the aforementioned 'hydro-supports' - hollow mountings internally divided into two chambers, with a small hole allowing antifreeze to flow between them, thus acting like a shock absorber. Combined with the contra-rotating balance shafts, the driver was left with the impression of a very smooth power unit.

The transaxle system found on the 924 and 928 was retained, albeit with relocated and modified mountings. As Bott said: "The Porsche transaxle principle is basically a compromise between the standard front engine, rear-wheel drive and the rear engine, rear drive layouts. Part of the drivetrain - the transmission - is separated from the front-mounted engine and located near the rear axle. This improves both handling and roadholding, particularly in the wet."

Like the 924 Turbo, the 944 employed a 25mm bar (running in three bearings) to take power to the rear axle, and a hydraulically-operated 225mm diameter clutch. The Getrag gearbox wasn't necessary to handle the level of horsepower developed by

*A cutaway drawing would usually be used to show a car's technical details and layout, but, thanks to the Porsche apprentices, for the 944 we have a cutaway vehicle, as displayed at the 1982 Geneva Show.*

*The five-speed manual gearbox in cutaway form. Note the linkage at the top of the unit.*

*The 944's front suspension and brakes.*

the 944 engine, so the Audi-derived transmission was specified, albeit with a strengthened input shaft.

Known as the 016J unit and built in Kassel, the internal ratios were 3.60, 2.12, 1.46, 1.07 and 0.83:1 (all but fourth and fifth gears being the same on the contemporary normally-aspirated 924), while the final-drive ratio was an equally familiar 3.89:1. In the 944, this gave intermediate speeds of 34, 58, 85 and 115mph, and a top speed of 137 (54, 93, 136, 184 and 220kph, respectively); a limited-slip differential could be specified, known as the M220 option in Porsche terms.

Alternatively, a three-speed automatic gearbox was also listed as an option, with internal ratios of 2.55, 1.45 and 1.00:1, respectively, while the final-drive was 3.08:1. With this type of transmission, designated the O-87M, the 0-60 time was naturally slower than that of the manual car, 9.6 seconds being the official figure quoted for a European specification 944. However, the top speed was unaffected, and fuel consumption was only 10% down on the five-speed model (it was actually marginally less thirsty around town).

The 944's independent suspension was a suitably uprated version of the 924's, featuring MacPherson struts with coil springs, lower wishbones and a 20mm (0.79in) anti-roll up front, while the rear suspension incorporated semi-trailing arms, transverse torsion bars and hydraulic dampers. A harder Sports suspension package was available as an option, which came with a pair of anti-roll bars, 21.5mm (0.85in) at the front, 14mm (0.55in) at the rear, although some markets were supplied with anti-roll bars at both ends as part of the standard specification.

The servo-assisted, dual-circuit

*A final shot of the Geneva show car, this view illustrating one of the driveshafts, and part of the rear suspension, braking system and exhaust. Careful observation reveals that even the Spacesaver spare didn't escape the cutaway treatment; it's standing upright in the well provided at the back of the vehicle. This picture also shows the reason why the luggage loading area was set so high.*

braking system came courtesy of the 924 Turbo, with Porsche ventilated discs all-round (283mm diameter at the front, 289mm at the rear, or 11.1 and 11.4in respectively), with the floating calipers coming off the 928. Like the 911's, the handbrake was via a drum built into the rear disc, a highly efficient arrangement. ABS wasn't offered initially as Porsche engineers weren't satisfied with the results obtained when testing the various systems on the market at the time. However, Helmuth Bott indicated that the Stuttgart firm was in the middle of developing its own anti-lock brakes, expected to become available in the near future.

The 944 was equipped with 7J x 15 cast alloys shod with 185/70 VR-rated tyres. 215/60 VR-rated Pirelli Cinturatos were available as an option on the 15 inch rim (M164), and forged 7J x 16 Fuchs alloys could also be specified, fitted with 205/55 VR16 Pirelli P7s (M458). A Spacesaver spare was standard, while the rack-and-pinion steering required 3.8 turns lock-to-lock; power-assisted steering was said to be in the pipeline.

Based on the floorpan and basic structure of the 924, physically, the body resembled that of the 924 Carrera GT but, instead of employing lightweight reinforced polyurethane for some of the panels, in the case of the 944, the coachwork was executed in steel throughout. Although this required additional tooling, from a

*A 944 prototype based on the 924 Carrera GT, and dating from 1980.*

volume production point of view, this was much better for a number of reasons, and the galvanising process enabled Porsche to supply the car with its standard seven-year, anti-perforation warranty - only the bumpers and wraparound front airdam were formed in 'Bayerflex' plastic. A rear spoiler was standard in all markets, moulded in black polyurethane and of the same deeper design as that on the Carrera GT.

Incidentally, like the 924 from the same period, the 944 came with a stronger roof than that of the earlier 924s, enabling it to adopt the new Porsche Carrier System range of roof-racks. This encompassed an assortment of boxes and attachments, allowing the owner to carry up to 165lbs (75kg) of additional luggage, or sporting kit such as skis or bicycles.

Another feature inherited from the 924 was the unusual way in which stale air was extracted from the cockpit. Ducts underneath the rear hatch drew air into channels which routed it into the doors. The air was then extracted through a concealed vent at the leading edge of each door, a natural low-pressure area when the car is moving at speed. This, it was claimed, not only kept the rear window clear of condensation, but also kept the doors warm in colder weather.

As for dimensions, the overall length of the vehicle was 4200mm (165.3in), the wheelbase was listed at 2400mm (94.5in), the width was 1735mm (68.3in), and the height was 1275mm (50.2in). The track was 1477mm at the front and 1451mm at the rear (58.2 and 57.1in, respectively), while ground clearance was 125mm (4.9in).

Inside, there was a lot that would have looked familiar to the 924 driver, especially if they had the 1981 or '82 model. The general layout was identical, with a similar fascia and centre console, and the same 2+2 seating arrangements - high-backed 911-type sports seats up front, and a sculptured, if rather cramped rear seat, the back of which carried the roller blind-style luggage cover, or alternatively, it could be folded down to increase load-carrying ability.

The 944 inherited the latest improved heating and ventilation system from the 924, carpeting to the centre console, a Porsche badge on the glovebox (to hide the lock) and embossed 'Porsche' script on the door cappings, and the new stalk design on the steering column.

There were some detail changes, of course. The VDO instruments featured revised graphics, marked up in yellow with yellow pointers. Like the 924, the main instrument binnacle housed a combined temperature and

*A rear view of the same machine. From a distance the bulging wings and large rear spoiler made the 944 look very similar to the 924 Carrera GT. Although the shape through the air wasn't as clean as a 924 Turbo, the Cd figure was lower than that of a standard 924, and aerodynamic lift was substantially reduced.*

*The 944 at the time of its announcement. Obvious differences between the 924 Carrera GT and the 944 include the lack of air intakes on the bonnet and nose panel, but careful inspection reveals a difference in the bumpers, too, the latter being designed to merge into the wraparound front apron to aid aerodynamics. Although the lines of the front wing and airdam were very similar, the spoiler had a bare minimum of openings, and the panel joints were far cleaner and much more suitable for a high quality production car.*

*Dashboard of an early 944 for the home market. The gearbox had a more traditional change pattern than that of the 924 Turbo, with fifth gear being up and to the right of the 'H' (reverse was below fifth). Note the standard three-spoke steering wheel and the Porsche badge on the glovebox.*

fuel gauge (which also contained most of the warning lights), a speedometer (with press-to-reset odometer), and a tachometer. However, the tachometer, red-lined at 6600rpm, despite the ignition cut-out coming into operation at least 100rpm lower, could be ordered with an optional auxiliary gauge for measuring fuel economy. In some countries, this was calibrated to show

*Left: A very early example, seen here fitted with the optional, and very expensive, 16-inch Fuchs alloys. Although these wheels looked the same as the Fuchs design found on the 911s, in fact, they had a different offset, so were therefore unique to the four-cylinder car. This is how the Type 944 went into production (it should be noted that although rhd cars were also sold under the 944 name, the official factory designation for the latter was Type 945).*

mpg figures, whilst in others it read in litres per kilometre. The switches for the lights, rear screen heater and hazard warning lights were also ahead of the driver, just below the main group of meters.

Like the 924, a 380mm (14.96in) three-spoke steering wheel was standard, with a leather-covered, four-spoke item, some 20mm (0.79in) smaller in diameter, listed as an option. Sadly, nothing was done about giving the column height and reach adjustment, so complaints from testers about there not being enough clearance between the wheel rim and the driver's thighs were still common.

The centre console played host to three auxiliary gauges - one for oil pressure, a clock, and a voltmeter for the battery. Below these were the heating controls (two fresh air vents in the centre of the dashboard, with another placed at each end of the moulded panel), a switch for the foglight, a cigar lighter, handbrake warning light (the handbrake was still positioned between the sill and the driver's seat) and the audio unit. Aft of the gearstick was another bank of minor switches and an ashtray.

Electric windows came as standard (the switches being situated on the door capping), as did heated and electrically-adjustable door mirrors, although full specifications changed from market-to-market. As for major options, in addition to the mechanical upgrades, there was air conditioning, various stereo packages and leather upholstery.

The 944 weighed in at 2596lbs (1180kg), incidentally, with distribution being split 49% front, 51% rear. With a Cd of 0.35, it was midway between the standard 924 and the highly-efficient shape of the 924 Turbo.

After being shown to the press

*Another view of the 944 dashboard, this time featuring the smaller four-spoke steering wheel. The switch between the radio and gearshift wasn't always fitted, but, in any case, it controlled the balance between the front and rear speakers.*

a couple of weeks after Le Mans, the 944's public debut came at the 1981 Frankfurt Show (held in September), with full-scale production beginning at the end of the year. Like the 924, it was built at the old NSU works in Neckarsulm, although - as with the turbocharged two-litre unit found in the 924 Turbo - the engine was produced in Zuffenhausen, built by hand at a rate of around 75 per day.

## The 944 reaches the market

Writing for *Road & Track*, the venerable Paul Frere made an interesting observation: "Some of the new models unveiled at the 1981 Frankfurt Motor Show were entirely new, while others were modifications of existing models. But almost all were engineered for better fuel economy without sacrificing performance."

"The Porsche 944, however, is an

*Like the 924, the 944 could be provided with a sunroof. It could be locked in a tilted position, or taken out completely (as seen here) and stowed away in the boot. This picture reveals the 'Porsche' script embossed in the door capping, and the electric window controls situated to the right of this.*

*The 4.8 cu.ft luggage capacity was acceptable for a sports car, especially if its owners chose their luggage carefully, and could be increased to 7.7 cu.ft with the rear seat folded. Note the roller blind attached to the back seat - a cheap and effective cover for the contents of the boot.*

> **Standard coachwork colours (1982 MY)**
> Mocha Black, Gabon Grey, Guards Red, Gambia Red, Mauritius Blue, Alpine White, Havana Brown.
>
> **Special coachwork colours**
> Pewter Metallic, Light Blue Metallic, Black Metallic, Ocean Green Metallic, Claret Metallic, Meteor Metallic, Diamond Silver Metallic.
>
> **Trim materials**
> Black, brown or beige leatherette with matching inlays. Alternatively, inlays could be in a chequered Pasha velour (grey/black or beige/brown), or Pinstripe velour (black with white or brown with beige); seat facings could also be supplied in beige/white or brown/white Berber cloth, or black, brown or beige leather as an option. Carpets came in black, brown or beige.

exception as neither its performance nor its fuel economy is claimed to be better than the Porsche 924 Turbo's. The principal difference is one of image and development potential."

Helmuth Bott went on record stating: "We wanted to get away from the volume car image that still affects the 924. And we needed a car that was better suited to the crucial American market, as it takes over a third of our production. On the other hand, we couldn't afford to produce a completely new model. It was clear from the beginning that the 944 would have to use as many components from other models as possible, but that it should differ visually from them as much as possible."

The timing may have been perfect, as Audi had just announced plans to market a more powerful 2.2 litre version of the Audi Coupé. Although it had cost some £27 million to develop, at least with the 944, Porsche now had a vehicle that could compete on equal terms with the new machine from Ingolstadt.

Peter Schutz was ecstatic; he said: "In my first year at Porsche, one of the things that has become clear is that it is not the optimum for us to build sports cars with other people's mass-production components. Now we have the 944 engine we plan to keep the Porsche line exclusive." A 2.5 litre four, with its inherent roughness, was unusual for a modern prestige car. Indeed, only Mitsubishi and Jeep had similar-sized four-cylinder lumps for passenger car applications. However, from a production point of view, it made perfect sense. At the end of the day, Porsche may be one of the most famous names in the car industry, but the company's resources were limited compared with the likes of Stuttgart neighbour, Daimler-Benz.

In European trim, the engine developed 163bhp at 5800rpm and 151lbft at 3000rpm. These figures represented a vast improvement over the standard 924, and were only 14bhp and 33lbft down on the 924 Turbo. However, the flat torque curve - and the low-speed flexibility that came with it - of the normally-aspirated 2.5 litre unit made life much easier for the driver than the peaky power one tends

*The car that appeared in the first 944 catalogue, but in a different setting. When the headlights were parked, the driver could still 'flash' oncoming traffic in daylight hours via the auxiliary spotlights set into the bumper.*

*Double-page spread from a French range brochure introducing the new 944. The side repeater lights on the front wing were the same design as those used on the contemporary 924s, by the way. To prevent fuel from getting on the coachwork, there was a drip flap behind the petrol cap.*

to experience with all turbocharged powerplants. The new engine was thus equally suited to manual and automatic transmission.

Another impressive feature was the power unit's low fuel consumption. According to official paperwork, the 944 was capable of 40.4mpg at a steady 56mph, 32.5 at a steady 75, and 24.8 for the urban cycle - all very impressive for a 137mph machine. With the manual 'box, the 0-60mph time was quoted at 8.4 seconds, but Porsche had always been conservative when it came to performance figures.

The 944 was well priced, too. Schutz wanted to sell the new car for around DM 35,000. Considering that the standard 924 was DM 30,980 at the time, the company's Finance Director, Heinz Branitzki, suggested DM 42,000 would be nearer the mark. Ultimately, this latest four-cylinder Porsche was launched at DM 38,900, although it must be said that by the summer it had already topped DM 40,000.

Initial press reaction was deep admiration. The *Autocar* noted: "Porsche set out to produce a large four-cylinder engine with close to six-cylinder levels of smoothness and refinement. They have not only succeeded in that aim, but have also produced perhaps the most relaxed and effective power unit of this size we have met in recent years ... What it lacks in sheer power, it gains in its wonderfully effective spread of torque."

Everyone raved about the ease with which rapid progress could be made, not to mention the exceptional handling. In Australia, Barry Lake said: "Only on very slippery surfaces or very tight corners will the back end break away due to power-induced wheelspin and then the quick, positive steering and the car's overall good manners makes it easy and highly-satisfying to get it all back into line." Following his test in Germany, George Kacher added: "The truth is, only a handful of cars hold the road as well in the wet as this Porsche can."

## Caractéristiques techniques

**Carrosserie :**
coupé 2 portes, 2 + 2, hayon arrière, sièges arrière rabattables.

**Moteur :**
4 cylindres en ligne, de 2,5 litres, refroidi par eau, arbre à cames en tête, entraîné par courroie crantée, avec 2 arbres compensateurs antivibration pour équilibrage des masses. Allumage électronique digital, injection BOSCH L-JETRONIC.

**Alésage :**
100 mm

**Course :**
78,9 mm

**Cylindrée :**
2479 ccm

**Rapport volumétrique :**
10,6 : 1

**Puissance :**
120 kW (163 ch DIN) à 5800 tr/mn

**Couple maxi :**
205 Nm à 3000 tr/mn (20,9 mkp)

**Transmission :**
boîte 5 vitesses
unité transaxle - moteur avant, boîte et pont arrière - réunis en unité rigide par tube central.

**Freins :**
4 freins à disque ventilés à l'intérieur, avec étrier flottant à l'avant et à l'arrière, servo-frein, système hydraulique à 2 circuits indépendants.

**Poids :**
poids à vide (DIN) : 1180 kg
poids total autorisé : 1500 kg

**Performances :**
accélération 0-100 km/h : 8,4 sec.
vitesse maxi : 220 km/h

**Consommation :** (Normes UTAC)
à 90 km/h, 7,0 litres aux 100 km
à 120 km/h, 8,7 litres aux 100 km
en ville, 11,4 litres aux 100 km.

Meanwhile, the respected journalist, Jerry Sloniger, wrote: "The car is richly fitted with such things as electric windows or optional air conditioning, along with stiffer shocks and a second anti-roll bar for the Sport package ... Since the torque of 151lbft peaks at 3000rpm and stays high over a wide range, the car pulls like a train in any gear, with little need for all 6500 revs.

"Standard 'box is a five-speed manual with top only slightly long so the 137mph (220kph) comes in fifth ... Without losing that sporting flavour - the engine has a far more pleasant exhaust tone - Porsche is promoting efficiency here, and reasonable transport, as chief 944 virtues. Given the performance they aren't likely to find many buyers paying attention. This is, quite simply, the engine and chassis we all wanted in a 924 from the first."

The 944 also scored highly in the ergonomics department, Kacher observing that "Visibility is good all round, the pedals are nicely weighted and ideally spaced, and the gearlever sprouts from the centre console at the optimum spot."

However, one of the few areas in which the 944 could be criticised was its lack of interior appointment. Some were so taken by the new package, true comparisons with the 924, that had recently been upgraded, were forgotten. As *Popular Classics* wrote some years later: "The 924's rather basic interior style grates when translated to the rather more expensive, upmarket 944. Efforts were made but the hard shiny plastic fascia, for instance, looks tacky and unworthy of the marque."

## The 944 in the UK

The gap between the 924 and 928 was narrowed for the 1982 model year when the 944 made its UK debut at the 1981 Earls Court Show, which opened on 21 October. Interest centred around the new Porsche, although it had to share some of the limelight with the futuristic De Lorean (another debutante), the

*An early 944 for the UK market, the third largest for Porsche after the USA and Germany. These were the standard 7J x 15 alloys provided for the 944, incidentally, shod with 185/70 rubber. In this picture, one can clearly see why many chose the wider tyres available on this rim in order to fill out the wheelarches a little better.*

Ford Fiesta XR2 hothatch, and a number of interesting competition cars.

The 944 went on sale in the UK at Easter 1982. It was priced at £12,999 for the five-speed manual, or £13,477 for the automatic. It was sold in Lux form only, and, as such, came with a fair amount of standard equipment: front and rear anti-roll bars (21.5mm and 14mm, respectively), a four-speaker Panasonic radio/cassette with electric aerial, headlight washers, tinted glass with electric window lifts, a rear wiper, and an electrically-adjustable driver's door mirror.

Oddly, like European counterparts, British spec cars also came with a Spacesaver spare, despite the law prohibiting them at the time. Fortunately, the powers that be eventually saw sense, and the problem was later resolved. It was provided with a jack, a small electric pump and tyre pressure gauge; there was also a decent toolkit for roadside repairs.

Writing for *Classic Cars*, Roger Bell noted at the time of the new model's UK launch: "What a remarkable car! An in-line four-cylinder engine displacing 2.5 litres sounds more like a recipe for a vibro-massage than a silken dream. Yet it is the turbine smoothness of the new Porsche 944's engine that makes the car so memorable.

"Like the engine, the gearchange is a gem, short and precise in travel with no baulking; clutch and throttle actions are also outstanding.

"Steering is sharper than that of the 924, due to fatter tyres and slightly higher gearing. Not surprisingly, it's also a bit heavier when parking. On the move though, the wheel is perfectly weighted and endearingly communicative, perhaps to the point where it tends to exaggerate the car's modest understeer when diving quickly into slow corners. On fast ones, the 944's grip and stability is pretty well flawless.

"So excellent are the qualities that really matter - performance, economy, refinement, comfort, build quality, finish - that the 944's few deficiencies seem rather trivial ... Even at £13,000, the five-speed manual does not appear to have a competitor in sight."

*MotorSport* thought the car equally praiseworthy. In the July 1982 issue it said: "Make no mistake about it, this is a 'proper' Porsche powered by a quite unbelievably smooth four-cylinder engine which could easily be mistaken for a six, or even a V8, from behind the steering wheel. This is combined with a chassis configuration that offers splendidly well-balanced handling and high level of grip, and levels of fuel economy which would have been deemed quite reasonable for a normal family saloon a few years ago. With a manual five-speed gearbox the Porsche 944 carries a price tag of £12,999 which, to put it very mildly, makes it very competitive indeed in that sector of the market.

"Porsche's policy of shrewd development and constant improvement will doubtless make the 944 an even better and more exciting car over the next few years. But, for the moment, you really do have to stretch your imagination to see how they're going to do it."

When *Autocar* tested the 944, it recorded a 0-60 time of 7.4 seconds, a 15.6 second standing-quarter and a top speed of 137mph (by the way, other contemporary tests gave almost identical results, *Motor* managing 0-60mph in 7.2). The magazine also returned a remarkable average of 26.2mpg - a fuel consumption figure one would usually associate with a two-litre family saloon of the time. Not surprisingly, *Autocar* described the car as "fast and very efficient," adding that it was also a "refined" vehicle.

On the minus side, the magazine was surprised by the amount of road noise: "Clearly one expects higher than average levels of road induced noise in a wide-tyred coupé like the 944, but we wonder if Porsche could not have done somewhat better in this respect, especially as mechanical refinement and exhaust silencing is so out of the ordinary." The testers were also a little disappointed with the heating and ventilation system, which was "slow to respond" and "difficult to modulate."

Options included air conditioning (£843), leather trim (£699), a sunroof (£350), metallic paint (£314), an electrically-adjustable door mirror for the passenger side (£105), the fuel consumption gauge mentioned earlier in the chapter (£70), a cassette holder (skilfully disguised as a centre armrest, priced at £70), a limited-slip differential (£385) and low-profile 215/60 VR15 tyres.

However, such was the poise of the new Porsche, the optional wider tyres were considered largely unnecessary by the majority of testers. *Alternative Cars* noted: "Given the high standards of roadholding, the impeccable handling and the refinement of the ride quality, the testing team felt that the optional 215/60 low-profile tyres could only bring a very slight improvement in standards that would be achieved at the expense of ride comfort and tyre noise. Given the unparalleled suppression of noise that makes the normally-shod 944 such an uncannily quiet car to drive, such a move would be unwise, for it would be a very demanding driver indeed who would have reason to sacrifice two of the 944's greatest strengths in pursuit of even higher levels of grip."

As for competitors, the 944 was up against cars like the Audi Quattro, the Lotus Esprit S3 and Eclat Excel, the TVR Tasmin, AC 3000ME, Alfa Romeo GTV and the Ford Capri 2.8i. The formidable Audi, priced at £15,037 had the advantage of four-wheel drive, but almost identical performance and significantly worse fuel consumption. The £13,513 Lotus had 160bhp in normally-aspirated form, a more than reasonable turn of speed, and the added kudos of having been selected to appear in the latest Bond movie, *For Your Eyes Only*.

The other British cars mentioned here were intended for a niche market, but the Alfa and Ford represented much more serious competition. The Alfa GTV, particularly in £10,250 GTV6 form, was a superb Grand Tourer.

Although even the six-cylinder version wasn't quite as quick as the Stuttgart machine, it was both practical and a true thoroughbred. The quick V6 Ford had a lot to offer over the 924, but while the performance gap was closed with the 944, the Cologne car's pricing (just £8125) only served to emphasize the evergreen Ford's magnificent value for money.

From Japan there was the Mazda RX-7, Toyota's new 2.8 litre Celica Supra, Nissan's 280ZX, and the Mitsubishi Colt Starion Turbo. All were cheaper than the Porsche, fast and reliable, and featured exceptional levels of standard equipment. The Mitsubishi was, perhaps, the closest in terms of performance, but was hardly pretty by any stretch of the imagination. The Saab 900 CD, BMW 728i and Mercedes-Benz 280CE offered interesting alternatives in the same price bracket, and Porsche's own 924 Turbo couldn't be dismissed.

Summing up, though, as a package, the 944 was hard to beat. Following its road test, the *Autocar* concluded: "The [Alfa Romeo GTV6] may just have an edge on mechanical refinement, but it is little if any better in this respect than the uncannily smooth-revving and more responsive Porsche. Over-riding all is the 944's out of the ordinary efficiency, handling and grip. It is superbly finished and has a unique balance of qualities that for

*British advertising for the 944, dating from May 1982.*

# A VERY POWERFUL NEW REASON FOR PARTING WITH AROUND £13,000.
# A VERY POWERFUL NEW PORSCHE.

The introduction of the 944 marks another milestone in the achievements of Porsche. For in the best tradition of Porsche development, it is not only the car that is new. It is the concept, too.

Consider the brief.

The 944 should marry the most advanced technology of the ultimate luxury sports car, the 928, with the equally acclaimed everyday practicality and economy of the 924.

The result, as might be expected, is the unexpected.

### A HIGH PERFORMANCE SPORTS CAR THAT IS NOT EXPENSIVE TO RUN.

The unexpected lies in an entirely new powerplant. It's pure Porsche. A 4 cylinder, 2½ litre unit that develops a hefty 120kw (163 bhp) at 5,800 rpm, yet turns in its peak torque of 205Nm at only 3,000rpm.

Its flexibility is outstanding. 190Nm at 2,000rpm, and on tickover, it's still producing 160Nm.

Put more simply, full blooded power is on tap when needed. And, more significantly, that power stays with you right through the rev range.

The 944 engine bristles with 928 technology. From the alloy cylinder head with the self adjusting tappets to the crankshaft lubrication system.

And there's something else, not new, but important. Contra rotating balance shafts that actually counter secondary engine vibration.

The upshot? A power drive that is smoother and quieter than anything ever achieved before by an engine of this configuration and performance.

### LEAN AND HUNGRY. THIRSTY, NO.

Equally unexpected is the economy. At a constant 56 miles per hour you can expect 40 miles or more per gallon. In heavy town traffic 25.* The automatic, even more.

How? By a virtuoso performance of aero and thermo dynamics. Aerodynamics that give a drag coefficient of just 0.35. Superior even to a 928S. Thermodynamics that cut fuel consumption to the bone. The 944's digital engine control system and fully electronic fuel system monitor, for example, 4,096 engine functions. So the economy goes on.

And on. With 12,000 miles between services and oil changes.

### IT EXHILARATES FROM 0-137.

And probably more. Without stress. Without strain.

For the sophisticated smoothness of the 944 is its most desirable feature. And when it comes to stopping, it does. Rapidly.

Ventilated discs all round bring you effortlessly from 62-0 in just 3.3 seconds. Because it's a Porsche it shows natural poise and balance. Achieved by even weight distribution. Engine fore. Gearbox aft.

And where others run roughshod the 944 runs with ease. Hugging the ground on low profile 911 tyres and wheels.

### IT'S NO MEAN MACHINE.

Rarely can sports motoring have looked a more attractive proposition. The 944 is unquestionably de luxe. Five star 2 + 2 accommodation, tinted glass, electrically operated exterior mirror, rear wiper, sophisticated stereo cassette radio, multi-speaker system, electric aerial. All standard.

As is the superior finish.

Optional is the automatic gearbox. But no soft option, this. The 944's outstanding torque qualities keep response razor sharp.

### AND A WORKHORSE TO BOOT.

The rear hatch conceals a veritable chasm. Room enough to carry the Louis Quinze escritoire.

Or, for the more sporting, a full size racing cycle.

And, again due to that remarkable engine, you'll find a 944 ideal for towing over a ton. Or carrying a roofload of 165 lbs. Add Porsche's unique 7-year 'leave it alone' anti-corrosion warranty, depreciation that's likely to be as slow as the car is quick, and you'll begin to see why the 944 is no ordinary car.

But don't take our word for it.

Drive one. Experience one. Relish one. Then you may come to the same conclusion as Georg Kacher of 'Car' magazine.

"Few sports cars combine performance and fuel economy the way this Porsche does ... the Porsche 944 is immensely rewarding to drive and makes a lot of sense to own."

We concur.

PORSCHE CARS GREAT BRITAIN LIMITED. Richfield Avenue, Reading RG1 8PH. Telephone: 0734 595411.

Tourist, NATO, Diplomatic, Personal Export Enquiries Tel: 0734 595411. Present Porsche line-up comprises: 4 cylinder 924 Series from £9,103; 4 cylinder 944 Series from £12,999; 6 cylinder 911 Series from £16,732; 8 cylinder 928 Series from £21,827. Prices, correct at going to press exclude number plates. *DoE Test: mpg (l/100km) 944 Auto: Urban: 25.2 (11.2), Constant 56mph: 35.8 (7.9), Constant 75mph: 30.1 (9.4). 944 5 speed: Urban: 24.8 (11.4), Constant 56mph: 40.4 (7.0), Constant 75mph: 32.5 (8.7). ■ SOUTH EAST: AFN, Isleworth 01-560 1011. AFN, Guildford 0483 38448. Charles Follett, Mayfair 01-629 6266. Motortune, Chelsea 01-581 1234. Malaya Garage, Billingshurst 040-381 3341. Maltin Car Concessionaires, Henley 04912 78111. ■ SOUTH WEST: Dick Lovett, Malborough 0672 52381. Parks, Exeter 0392 32145. ■ SOUTH: Heddell & Deeks, Bournemouth 0202 510252. ■ MIDLANDS: Swinford Motors (Continental) Ltd., Lye 038-482 2471. Roger Clark, Narborough 0533 848270. Gordon Lamb Chesterfield 0246 451611. Monarch Cars (Warwick) Ltd., Warwick 0926 491731. ■ EAST ANGLIA & ESSEX: Lancaster Garages, Colchester 0206 48141. Lancaster Garages, Norwich 0603 401814. ■ NORTH WEST: Ian Anthony, Wilmslow 0625 526392. Ian Anthony, Bury 061-761 2222. Parker & Parker, Kendal 0539 24331. ■ NORTH EAST: JCT 600, Leeds 0532 508454. Gordon Ramsay, Newcastle-upon-Tyne 0632 612591. ■ WALES: Howells, Cardiff 0222 592363. Dingle Garages, Colwyn Bay 0492 30456. ■ SCOTLAND: Glen Henderson, Ayr 0292 82727. Glen Henderson, Glasgow 041-943 1155. Glen Henderson, Edinburgh 031-225 9266. ■ NORTHERN IRELAND: Isaac Agnew, Glengormley 02313 7111. ■ CHANNEL ISLANDS: Jones Garage, Jersey 0534 26156.

*In racing, 1982 was the year in which the Group C gladiators entered the scene, so the all-new 956 tended to overshadow the three less glamorous 924 Carrera GTRs entered at Le Mans. However, Jim Busby and Doc Bundy (seen here) finished first in Class and 16th overall, 87 laps down on the winning Porsche. This was the 924 derivative's last appearance at the Sarthe track.*

the price makes the few niggles seem utterly insignificant."

## The new car in America

Compared to vehicles like the best-selling RX-7, the 924, at almost $17,000 in basic trim, was far too expensive in the USA, pricing itself off the market. With the prevailing exchange rates, to sell it any cheaper, however, would have meant little or no profit, so, after a few months, the 944 - which provided a better return - was the only four-cylinder Porsche listed for America's 1982 model year, arriving there in spring to be sold as an early 1983 model.

For the American market, where the engines carried the M44/02 designation (or M44/04 if automatic transmission was specified), compression ratio was lowered slightly to 9.5:1. This, combined with a three-way catalytic converter and all the other paraphernalia necessary to meet exhaust gas regulations, such as the oxygen sensor fitted to all Porsches bound for the States since 1980, naturally resulted in a drop in power and dictated the use of unleaded fuel only. The US spec models were listed with 143bhp (at 5500rpm) and 137lbft of torque, the latter coming in at 3000rpm, although 944s headed Stateside displayed the same wonderfully flat torque curve as that found on European counterparts.

A five-speed manual gearbox was standard, although it was slightly different to the one sold in Europe. Carrying the 016K appellation, top gear was listed at 0.73 instead of 0.83:1

(the Japanese market also received this revised gearing); the back axle, meanwhile, had the same 3.89:1 final-drive ratio. The automatic transmission option (type O-87N) came with a 3.45:1 final-drive, incidentally.

US cars were shod with 215/60 VR15 tyres, mounted on the 7J x 15 rim; the 16-inch wheels and tyres were listed as an option, as was a Sports suspension package. The latter included stiffer shock absorbers, a 21.5mm anti-roll bar at the front and a 14mm diameter bar at the rear (a 20mm bar at the front only was provided as standard in the States).

Announced at a base price of $18,450 (although it soon rose to just under $19,000), as usual, it had side markers (far more elegant than those seen previously), and slightly different bumpers to comply with Federal law, thus adding 120mm (4.7in) to the car's overall length. These larger bumpers and the obligatory exhaust emissions control equipment increased the 944's kerb weight by about 190lbs, or 87kg, taking it to a figure not dissimilar to that of the Federal spec 924 Turbo.

Air conditioning, a sunroof, electric door mirrors and windows (with tinted glass) were all part of the standard package, as were foglights and leather trim to the three-spoke steering wheel and gearknob. Major options included leather upholstery ($950), bucket sports seats ($250), various stereo upgrades (a basic Blaupunkt radio and electric aerial was provided in the standard specification), and so on.

Road noise, poor ventilation (despite Porsche claiming a 10% improvement in output there were still a few grumbling journalists), and the low mounting of the steering wheel, which lacked any kind of adjustment, were bugbears inherited from the 924. Some also pointed out the rather fierce brakes, leading a few to suggest they were perhaps a little over-servoed. On the whole, however, most testers came away from this latest four-cylinder Porsche with a very good impression.

Having recorded a 0-60 time of 8.3 seconds and a 16.3 second standing-quarter, *Road & Track* was very enthusiastic about the 944's powerplant, and, indeed, the car in general: "You'll find that the engine fires up immediately and runs smoothly, even when cold. And Lordy, does it rev - right up to the red-line in every gear except fifth. There are no stumbles, flat spots or resonance points. Furthermore, there's low- and mid-range flexibility that allows you to drop the revs to as low as 1000rpm in top gear and the engine pulls without protest.

"The 944 is one of the most exciting cars to come out of Zuffenhausen (by way of Neckarsulm) in a long time. It is spirited, yet smooth. It handles superbly, yet its ride is not harsh. It has swoopy looks, period."

Braking, handling and roadholding were of an exceptionally high order, but more than one journalist warned that once the 944 did reach its breakaway point, it required "the same sort of quick and competent reaction as the 911" to keep it on the road. However, few would ever even approach the limits of the new Porsche. As *Road & Track*

commented: "The 944 has a neutral feel and a tendency toward power understeer. Throttle lift-off brings the tail out, but ever so slightly and controllably."

In a *Motor Trend* article, the 944 was compared with the 924 Turbo on the test track. The two cars were very similar through the slalom, although it

*American advertising from the summer of 1982. Note the different rear bumper to that used on European models, and the obligatory side marker.*

*A slightly later US advert describing the technology behind Porsche's new engine. Again, note the different bumper and side marker (fortunately, far prettier than those found on the 924s), and the standard foglamps. European cars could also be ordered with foglights, which were fitted in a modified front apron produced purely for that purpose.*

this engine; the curve is almost flat from 3000rpm to 5500rpm, peaking as early as 3000rpm when it reaches 151lbft and never falling below 138lbft between 2500 and the 6400rpm red-line."

By July 1982, due to the popularity of the 944, production of the 924 Turbo had officially ceased, although some were still being built for the Italian market, where the exorbitant tax on vehicles with engines over two litres (it rose from 18% to 35%) made it a viable proposition, until the end of 1983.

Despite a late introduction, it was the 944 that was Porsche's top seller Stateside in 1982. Accounting for 5125 (or 37%) of the 13,748 sales made that year in America (not including tourist deliveries), the 944 also helped push up the annual total, as it had been only 11,241 units in 1981. Total Porsche production for 1982 was 31,734 vehicles, incidentally.

was easier to get the most from the new model, and they were neck and neck throughout all of the performance tests (the 2.5 litre machine clocking a 0-60 time of 7.74 seconds, incidentally). The only area in which there was a significant difference was braking, where the fatter tyres on the 944 gave it an advantage of around 7% over its turbocharged cousin. All told, the results were very admirable.

Even Paul Frere, a staunch supporter of the 911, was impressed. In the April 1982 issue of *Road & Track*, he noted: "The car is a lot quicker than advertised. The engine is beautifully smooth, silent and torquey; and the gearchange and the steering are better than the 911's - the steering mainly because it suffers from much less kickback. Porsche can certainly be proud of the torque characteristics of

# 4
## THE EARLY PRODUCTION MODELS

At the start of 1983, while most manufacturers were struggling (Volkswagen made heavy losses in 1982 and 1983), Porsche was booming. The Zuffenhausen works was building around 75 cars a day (55 911s to 20 928Ss), whilst the Neckarsulm factory, which was still being rented from Volkswagen, was producing about 105: 80 944s and 25 924s.

Schutz was fulfilling his promise to revive the 911 - a Cabriolet version was shown at the 1982 Geneva Show - and in 1983 the range acquired a new 3164cc engine. With 231bhp on tap (a jump of 27bhp over the already increased 1980 outputs), these models were given the Carrera appellation, making a perfect complement to their 3.3 litre Turbo stablemate. The standard 928 was dropped in the reshuffle, with the 928S carrying the mantle for the series.

It was around this time that Dr Helmut Kohl replaced Helmut Schmidt as Germany's Chancellor (basically, head of the German government). Schmidt had done a sterling job in bringing the country through a series of oil shocks and currency crises, although unemployment continued to rise during the 1980s. An interesting development was the rise of the Greens, an environmentalist party. With the car a major target for their scorn, what would this mean in the future?

### The 1983 model year

For the 1983 model year proper (introduced on the first day of October 1982), synchromesh was added to the reverse gear on the five-speed transaxle, and the O-87M automatic gearbox was also modified, with the lower ratios being altered slightly to give better acceleration. At the same time, the camshaft and balance shaft drives were improved in the hope of extending the life of the two toothed belts employed at the front of the engine. Other minor changes included covers for the door speakers.

In Britain, the 944 cost £13,390 at this time, although, due to a hefty DM 1400 price increase in Germany, by the summer of 1983 the 944 had shot up some £1579. The standard 924 was still listed, but, for comparison purposes, it's perhaps better to quote the £9993 of the 924 Lux, as the basic version was hardly ever supplied. Automatic transmission was £499 extra on both models.

Bill Boddy, long-serving editor of *MotorSport*, tried a 944 for size. Although he felt the steering was "a trifle low-geared" and "not as precise as I had expected," he was still very impressed. He commented: "The comfort, performance and high quality of the Porsche 944 reminded me of F.L.M. Harris, motoring writer of the 1920s, remarking, of the then new 12/50 Alvis, that it was the kind of car you took out just for the sheer pleasure of driving it - I felt just the same about the 944.

"It may seem pedantic to call a Porsche the 'Rolls-Royce of Fast Cars' but it is unquestionably a very desirable property and if I were a rich man I would be off to Reading [Porsche GB's headquarters] to order one."

The high regard with which the

> **Standard coachwork colours (1983 MY)**
> Black, Pasadena Yellow, Guards Red, Copenhagen Blue, Alpine White.
>
> **Special coachwork colours**
> Pewter Metallic, Sienna Red Metallic, Montego Black Metallic, Moose Green Metallic, Gemini Grey Metallic, Sable Brown Metallic, Sapphire Metallic, Light Bronze Metallic, Zermatt Silver Metallic.
>
> **Trim materials**
> Black, brown or grey-beige leatherette with matching inlays. Alternatively, inlays could be in a chequered Pasha velour (grey/black or grey-beige/brown), or pinstripe velour (black with white, brown with beige or grey-beige with white); seat facings could also be supplied in grey/black, beige/brown or grey-beige/brown Berber cloth, or black, brown or grey-beige leather as an option. Carpets came in black, brown, grey-beige or grey.

944 was held in America is obvious from the comparison test carried out by *Road & Track*, pitting it against the Chevrolet Corvette, Ferrari 308GTBi qv and the Porsche 928S - the fastest street legal production car available in the States at that time. Although the Italian supercar and the V8 Porsche were vastly more expensive (at $53,745 and $43,000, respectively), at $21,800, the Corvette was only $2315 more than the smaller Stuttgart machine.

It was a fascinating clash, confirming that each had a very different character. Way behind in the displacement stakes, the 944 naturally lagged behind the cars gathered for the article in outright speed, "but don't think the 944 had to take its lumps in this comparison test. A well rounded personality has a lot to do with its competitiveness. The engine is smaller than the others but provides excellent throttle response and good power for its size. Not as fast as the others, the 944 is still an entertainingly quick car. Steering provides a nice balance between road feel and road shock, not as sublime as the Ferrari's, but an equal to the 928's. Gearshift action is nearly as nice as the Ferrari's (better, cold) and far better than the 928's. On the highway or the race track, the 944 is an immensely nimble car with a good balance (there's that word again) among brakes, steering and cornering attitude. As already cited, the 944 produced the best slalom time of all the cars in the test."

The 944 got the most points in the subjective ratings, but the final verdict was split into two sections - a money-no-object and a price-dependent decision. In the latter category, perhaps not surprisingly, the 944 won hands down, gaining 12 points, five more than the Ferrari, six more than its

*The 944 in Guards Red, one of the most popular paintwork shades for the model. Note the colour-coded trim running along the waistline (between the two wheelarches only) that became a standard fitment in the UK for 1983. Options fitted to this German-registered car include the 16-inch Fuchs forged alloys, front foglights, and an alarm (witnessed by the small keyhole by the door handle).*

*Interior of the 1983 model year 944, clearly showing the 2+2 seating arrangement. It has to be said that making cloth door trim panels an option on such an expensive car was a little naughty; this car has the standard vinyl-covered items.*

*Like the 924 before it, the 944 also found service as a fast response vehicle for medics covering the German autobahns.*

German stablemate, and seven more than the 'Vette. Disregarding price, the Modena car scored 11, whilst the 944 was awarded eight points (one more than the 928S and twice what the Chevrolet was given).

During 1983, Porsche sales increased by over 50% in the States, thanks to the popularity of the 944. Establishing a new record, the Stuttgart marque sold a total of 21,831 units for the year, a figure

*A works publicity photo of the 1984 944.*

*A fascinating picture taken by the German motoring journal, Auto Zeitung, following a strip-down after a 31,000 mile (50,000km) road test.*

*Interior of the 1984 MY 944. The model benefited from a number of improvements, such as an internal release for the rear hatch and, when specified, electrical operation of the sunroof. Note the speaker covers on the door, introduced in 1983, and the optional cassette and coin holder situated aft of the centre console.*

> **Standard coachwork colours (1984 MY)**
> Black, Pasadena Yellow, Guards Red, Copenhagen Blue.
>
> **Special coachwork colours**
> Pewter Metallic, Ruby Red Metallic, Montego Black Metallic, Gemini Grey Metallic, Sable Brown Metallic, Sapphire Metallic, Light Bronze Metallic, Zermatt Silver Metallic.
>
> **Trim materials**
> Black, brown or grey-beige leatherette with matching inlays. Alternatively, inlays could be in a chequered Pasha velour (grey/black or grey-beige/brown), or pinstripe velour (black with white, brown with beige or grey-beige with white); seat facings could also be supplied in black, brown or grey-beige 'Porsche' cloth or leather as an option. Carpets came in black, brown, grey-beige or grey.

which represented about 46% of production.

## The 1984 model year

The big news for Porsche fans was the introduction of the four-wheel drive 959 supercar, first shown at the 1983 Frankfurt Show. The twin-turbo 2.9 litre engine produced no less than 450bhp, endowing the Group B monster with a 0-60 time of 3.9 seconds, and a top speed approaching 200mph. However, only 200 were made, priced at DM 420,000 (ten times the cost of a 944!).

As far as the 944 was concerned, steering was now power-assisted on automatic cars, and would soon be available as an option on those with manual gearboxes. This not only meant less effort was required when parking, but an 18.5:1 ratio instead of 22:1 also gave quicker steering response - only 3.2 turns lock-to-lock compared to 3.8.

The rear hatch was provided with an internal electric release (several contemporary tests highlighted how difficult it could be to get the key in underneath the spoiler), and the sunroof was now power operated. The fuel economy gauge was standard in some markets, whilst a useful addition for all cars was the brake

*Another view of the 1984 model year 944, seen here equipped with the optional Fuchs forged alloy wheels. Although most enthusiasts seem to hold up Guards Red as the ultimate 944 colour, the author prefers the more elegant metallic shades offered at the time.*

wear indicator, especially in view of the rapid deterioration of the front pads that most seemed to experience.

Lubrication was improved in the block, and new seals were fitted to the balance shafts following a number of complaints about oil leaks; soon after, the shields protecting the offside engine mount were redesigned. This modification was introduced because the heat from the exhaust was wreaking havoc with the fluid inside the rubber mounting, destroying its effectiveness and allowing the engine to vibrate. It was hoped that by getting more air around the mounting, the problem would be solved.

Although the car was slowly but surely being improved in typical Porsche fashion, the price was rising at a steady rate. In March 1983, the 944 had stood at DM 41,830, but a DM 1100 increase in August, and then another DM 1000 added in February 1984 saw it retailing at DM 43,950 before any options were added. A few months later, it was a hefty DM 45,350!

In the UK, the 1984 model year five-speed 944 was priced at £15,309 (by April 1984, the 944 was up to £16,074), while the 911 ranged from £21,464 to £33,878; the 928S S2, the only 928 available in Britain at the time, was listed at £30,679. As a matter of interest, the 924 was £11,495.

Judging by the long list of options available on the latter, and the relatively high base price, it's easy to see why 924 sales were steady rather than brisk. There was certainly a lot of competition on the market, and even stronger rivals would continue to filter through as the years progressed. Not surprisingly, given that this was supposed to be the volume seller, rumours started to circulate about the future of the smaller four-cylinder model.

The 944, however, continued to sell very well, the UK providing Porsche with its third biggest market after America and Germany. The accompanying table (overleaf) has the 944 section of the Porsche GB price list for the 1984 model year, highlighting several new options.

A number of specials were produced for the European market during 1984, by the way. Over the Easter period, 200 cars were built for Switzerland - 100 in black and the same amount in Zermatt Silver Metallic, both finished with black pinstripe interiors. At the same time, a further 100 were allocated for France, painted in white

## UK price list - September 1983

944 Lux Coupé .................................................................................................................................£15,308.80
944 Lux Coupé three-speed Automatic.............................................................................................£15,871.92

*Standard UK specification includes:*
Five-speed manual transmission
Light alloy 7J x 15 road wheels with 185/70 VR15 tyres
Front and rear anti-roll bars
Additional driving lamps mounted in front bumper
High intensity rear fog lamps
Brake pad wear indicator
Heated rear window
Two-speed windscreen wipers, intermittent wipe setting and electrically operated windscreen washers
Headlamp washers
Rear window wiper
Electrically operated door windows
Tinted, heat insulating glass
Heated and electrically adjustable driver's door mirror
Leather covered sport steering wheel (360mm diameter)
Fuel economy gauge
Body side protection mouldings
Lockable fuel filler cap
National Panasonic digital self-seek stereo radio with combined auto-reverse stereo cassette player (10W per channel) with Dolby and metal tape facilities, four speakers and automatic electric aerial
Rear compartment luggage cover
Electrically operated rear hatch release

*Optional equipment:*
Forged alloy road wheels with anti-theft device:
    Front: 7J x 15 wheels with 215/60 VR15 low-profile tyres
    Rear: 8J x 15 wheels with 215/60 VR15 low-profile tyres ...............................................................£748.74
Forged alloy road wheels with anti-theft device:
    Front and rear: 7J x 16 wheels with 205/55 VR16 low-profile tyres ..............................................£1124.99
215/60 VR low-profile tyres on standard road wheels ........................................................................£158.22
Forged alloy road wheel centres painted Grand Prix White or Pewter Metallic...................................£169.43
Front and rear anti-roll bars (large diameter) with sport shock absorbers..........................................£161.95
Limited-slip differential (manual transmission only) ...........................................................................£459.71
Integral front fog lamps .......................................................................................................................£109.63
Heated and electrically adjustable passenger door mirror ..................................................................£105.89
Burglar alarm system...........................................................................................................................£149.50
Removable sunroof panel with electric tilt facility ...............................................................................£560.63
Air conditioner.....................................................................................................................................£959.30
Anti-theft device for wheels (locking wheel nut) ...................................................................................£36.13
Leatherette sport seats with 'Porsche' cloth seat inlays - pair .............................................................£241.70
Leatherette sport seats with 'Porsche' cloth seat inlays and bolsters - pair ........................................£331.40
Standard seats with 'Porsche' cloth seat inlays and bolsters - pair ......................................................£89.70
Leather sport seats - pair ....................................................................................................................£877.07
Partial leather front seats (facings only) - pair....................................................................................£275.33
Cloth door panel facings with velour check or pinstripe trim ...............................................................£68.52
Cassette and coin holder ......................................................................................................................£73.51
Metallic paint .......................................................................................................................................£394.93

*The contemporary 924, with its smaller rear spoiler (by now standard) and optional multi-spoke alloy wheels.*

(a colour not actually listed for '84) with a black trim.

## US update

In America, the Bosch ignition and fuel-injection control system was revised for 1984 (now given the LE-Jetronic designation, although engine performance figures were identical), and power-assisted steering became

*A French-registered 944 in a suitably grand setting. The aerial on top of the front wing was rather unsightly when in the raised position, but an ingenious solution was in the pipeline.*

*Another picture of the French 944 on its tour of Europe. Note the standard wheels.*

*Below: American advertising from the period, this particular piece featuring a cutaway drawing of the 944's four-cylinder engine.*

standard. At the same time, cruise control and an electric sunroof were added to the options list (the roof panel could still be removed and stowed in the boot, incidentally).

A standard 944 had won the Longest Day of Nelson Ledges (an important 24-hour Showroom Stock event held annually at the Ohio race track) in 1982, but in 1984, the flag fell before a prototype 944 Turbo. Driven by Porsche veteran Jim Busby, Rick Knoop and Freddy Baker, it finished 42 laps ahead of the rest of the field, and gave the public a good idea of what was to come in the near future; the more freely-available, normally-aspirated 944, filled the second, fourth and fifth slots. Ironically, shortly after, an article appeared in *Road & Track*, gathering together eight of the best vehicles eligible for the SCCA Showroom Stock GT category - the Chevrolet Camaro Z28 and Corvette, the Dodge Daytona Turbo Z, Ford Mustang GT, Mazda's RX-7 GSL-SE, the Nissan 300ZX Turbo, Pontiac Firebird TransAm, and the 944. Prices ranged from around $10,000 to $23,360 (for the 'Vette), with the Porsche listed at $21,440.

Conducted at the Willow Springs race track, the 944 seemed to be in the middle of the field in each segment of this particular test, being close to the top of the table in top speed down the straight and under braking. The Porsche was described as an "impressive car," but it was the Corvette that shone on the day, leading the way in four out of six disciplines covered in the article. Nonetheless, the 944 was still named as one of Road & Track's '12 Best Enthusiast Cars of 1984', classed as the top Sports/GT model in the $18,000-$25,000 price sector. As a matter of interest, the Chevrolet Corvette was runner-up, with the Nissan 300ZX Turbo third.

*Car & Driver* was equally full of praise. To find the best-handling car in the States, it compared the 944 with the Camaro Z28 which, admittedly, was $10,000 cheaper, but a superb machine nevertheless. Larry Griffin observed: "The 944 is not viceless, but its pluses overwhelm its minuses. I'm nuts about the steering effort, the sureness of the brakes, and the precise tidiness of the chassis. Yes, it moves right and left in a straight line from time to time, but 98% of the time it's telling me what I want to know and reminding me why I want to know it."

Summing up, the *C&D* team said: "The Porsche is by no means perfect, but the two most important handling ingredients are baked deep within its soul: a fine balance of all the components that make the car go, turn and stop, and an unshakable dynamic poise. May the 944 have a long and fruitful reign as the best-handling automobile in all the land."

The obvious enthusiasm that specialist publications had for the 944 was reflected in its sales, and 924/944 production at Neckarsulm was increased to 135 units a day to meet demand, with the 2.5 litre model accounting for most of the output.

## A return to F1

After a few outings towards the end of 1983, the Porsche-built 1.5 litre turbocharged TAG engine won the first race of the 1984 Formula One season, and, combined with the McLaren chassis, the twin-turbo V6 went on to dominate for the rest of the year.

The commission had originally come in 1981. The TAG engine project was financed completely by the massive Techniques d'Avant Garde concern, and although Hans Mezger was responsible for its development, the specifications were basically decided by McLaren. Only a tiny 'Made by Porsche' label proclaimed its source, but there is no doubt that Porsche benefited from its success and the additional experience gained.

Excellent results came in 1984 and 1985 (by which time the unit was pushing out the best part of 1000bhp), but the Honda era had well and truly arrived during the following season - although McLaren's Alain Prost won the Drivers' Championship, Williams-Honda won the constructors' title by a convincing margin.

## The 944 for 1985

As 1985 approached, power-assisted steering was fitted across the entire 944 range in Europe (it had previously been batched together with the automatic transmission option, and listed as an extra on five-speed cars), but the model was finally starting to attract its fair share of critics.

Even by Britain's standards, where, for some reason, prices have always been slightly higher than those on the Continent, £16,880 was a lot to pay for a car at the time; adding on a few popular options (such as metallic paint at £444, a £123 passenger-side door mirror, or an electric sunroof at £664) soon sent the cost to the customer soaring.

Writing for *Classic Cars*, Brian Palmer found the engine to be very impressive, with something of a "dual character" (the driver was able to freely choose between performance or effortless progress, thanks to the unit's "exceptionally flat torque curve" and "extreme flexibility"), and he adored the shape. Overall, it must be said that he was obviously impressed with the package, as he summed up his article with these words: "Porsche use 'Driving in its Finest Form' as their slogan and it is particularly apt when applied to the 944."

However, Palmer questioned the 944's value-for-money, and noted the following: "Wind noise is commendably low which perhaps only serves to emphasize road roar from the low-profile tyres [another expensive option, incidentally]. On coarse surfaces, notably concrete sections of the motorway, this can set up a quite disturbing frequency which the body amplifies. The suspension, though admirable in all other respects, is poor in bump-thump absorption ... Of

*The 1985 model year 944 with its headlights raised. Thanks to the transaxle, traction in poor road conditions like this, whilst not as good as that of the 911 (with its weight biased over the rear, driven wheels), was much better than that of the majority of its contemporaries.*

course, Porsche deliberately set their cars' suspension characteristics for maximum handling and grip together with little roll. However, for the comfort of passengers, they could take a leaf out of the book of Hethel or even Brown's Lane when it comes to ride/handling compromise."

Just as faults with the car were beginning to be found, Porsche was ready with an answer. In December 1984, a number of changes were

*The same car in a very different setting.*

*An atmospheric shot from the mid-1980s.*

announced for the 944 to distance it further from the much cheaper entry-level 924. One of the most noticeable differences was the new dashboard. The main instrument binnacle was extended in an oval shape to house the two central air vents (as before, another smaller vent was situated at each end of the fascia), and some of the switches and controls were moved from the centre console to a largely flat panel between the top roll and lower dash trim, the latter providing the latest location for the lockable glovebox. As a consequence, the fusebox and

*A 1985 944 with 15-inch Fuchs alloys and locking wheel nuts. That year, there was a new 16-inch forged alloy wheel option consisting of 7J rims with 205/55 VR-rated tyres up front, and 8J x 16s with 225/50 VR16s at the back, while those customers who opted for painted centres on the forged alloys could now choose between Grand Prix White or Gold Metallic, the latter shade superseding Pewter Metallic. This picture shows the traditional - and vastly more popular - matt black centre.*

*The new 944 interior, available on the home market from January 1985, and elsewhere from spring that year. The 924 models continued to use the original dashboard, a design that was basically unchanged since the car's introduction a decade earlier.*

*Another view of the latest interior; this particular car is fitted with electrically-adjustable seats. Note the new door furniture and centre console.*

*The latest 'Telephone Dial' alloy wheels certainly gave the 944 a more modern look. Note the tail graphics - the familiar '944' badge was usually there in one form or another above the right-hand rear combination light, though owners could choose not to have it fitted.*

*Pages 84 & 85: This US advert from mid-1985 shows the earlier style windscreen and rain channel arrangement, due for an update in all markets for the 1986 model year. Judging by the text, this car has the new dashboard, however, and is fitted with the 15-inch version of the optional Fuchs forged alloy wheels shod with 215/60 VR-rated rubber.*

# Fun may be the most i

When Roland Kussmaul is tired of meetings, tired of wearing a tie, tired of hearing his phone ring, he leaves his office in the racing compound a few hundred yards west of the test track, to do the one thing he never gets tired of doing.

Driving.

Not driving as people who wear ties know it. But driving as Kussmaul knows it.

Putting the car a little bit sideways.

Kussmaul is a professional test driver. Which means he can detect a millimeter's difference in the thickness of a sway bar or a 5% adjustment in a spring rate. In a single test lap.

Kussmaul was Project Leader for our customer-owned 956 race cars. Project Manager on our SCCA 944

# portant discipline of all.

racer. And when he isn't helping tune the suspension of the Paris/Dakar 4-wheel drive car, he's out crossing African deserts in one.

Needless to say, a man like Roland Kussmaul isn't easily entertained.

Which says something about the Porsche 944.

A car Kussmaul drives not because it can do 0 to 60 mph in 7.2 seconds.

Not because its transaxle design helps make it the best handling production sports car on the market. Even when driven to Kussmaul's limit.

And no, not for its newly designed, 928-like interior.

But for what may be the best reason of all to drive any Porsche.

The fun of it.

**944** *4-cylinder, in-line, single overhead camshaft, liquid-cooled, front-engine, 2479cc's, 143 hp., transaxle. Weight: 2778 lbs. Top speed: 130 mph.*

> **Standard coachwork colours (1985 MY)**
> Black, Pastel Beige, Guards Red, Copenhagen Blue, Alpine White.
>
> **Special coachwork colours**
> Graphite Metallic, Garnet Red Metallic, Kalahari Metallic, Stone Grey Metallic, Crystal Green Metallic, Sapphire Metallic, Mahogany Metallic, Zermatt Silver Metallic.
>
> **Trim materials**
> Black, brown, burgundy or light grey leatherette with matching inlays. Alternatively, inlays could be in pinstripe velour (black with white, brown with beige, burgundy with white or grey with white); seat facings could also be supplied in pinstripe flannel cloth (in the same shades as the velour inlays), black, brown, burgundy or light grey 'Porsche' cloth or leather as an option. Carpets came in black, brown, burgundy or grey.

relays were moved into the engine compartment. Rather than hooded instruments, the new layout had what appeared to be four circles on the same plane contained within the oval feature. From left to right was the temperature gauge, fuel gauge, speedometer (with odometer), tachometer and economy gauge (and gear indicator on automatic models), an oil pressure gauge, and a voltmeter; all were marked in white and red with red pointers.

Beyond the four-spoke steering wheel, the switchgear on the column was brought up-to-date, with minor switches placed on either the slim, horizontal, central panel (which also carried the heating controls and a digital clock), or the centre console which, although modified to suit the new dashboard, still contained the audio equipment (the aerial was now embedded in the windscreen, incidentally). The door trim panels were also revised slightly to match the fascia, with new window switches, a tiny joystick for the mirrors, larger door pockets and different door release handles.

At the same time, the car's electrics, air conditioning system, and, indeed, the heating and ventilation in general, were all vastly improved. Airflow into the cabin was said to be up to one-third better than before, mainly due to the larger vents used, but the optional air con unit and standard heater were also far more efficient. The latter had thermostatic control, allowing the driver to select a set temperature, but of course, on hot days, there was no substitute for air conditioning. With both systems, there was a four-speed fan and recirculating facility.

Other improvements inside included a new automatic gearshift lever, and lowering the seat by 30mm (1.18in), whilst raising the steering column slightly to give an additional 19mm (0.75in) of thigh clearance; a small but noticeable difference. Another niggling problem was also addressed - the wipers on rhd cars now parked towards the nearside after years of complaints that unswept areas of the screen remained in the line of vision. Latest options included central locking and heated front seats, which could also be supplied with electrical adjustment.

Outside, the main distinguishing feature was the new 928-style 7J x 15 cast alloy wheel design, which came shod with 195/65 VR15 rubber. These were now classed as standard equipment on the 944, thus replacing the original five-spoke items. Under the skin was improved undersealing to combat the onslaught of corrosion, and a bigger fuel tank with a closed-loop breathing system. The latter had a 17.6 gallon (80 litre) capacity, some 3.1 gallons (14 litres) more than before, and was produced in plastic instead of steel.

Mechanically, the power unit received an enhanced engine management system, a modified combustion chamber, and revised pistons and exhaust valves. Oil capacity was increased from 1.21 gallons (5.5 litres) to 1.32 gallons (6 litres), which necessitated the use of a new oil pump, and the coolant capacity (formerly 1.87 gallons, or 8.5 litres) was also enlarged slightly via a different radiator.

As a result of these modifications, the engine - which was given uprated mountings - was now designated type M44/05, or 06 if equipped with automatic transmission; in the US, where the changes filtered through a little later, the numbers were 07 for five-speed cars and 08 for the three-speed, two-pedal models. Power and torque figures were the same as before in Europe but, as will be seen in the next chapter, they went up fractionally in the States.

The final batch of revisions applied to the suspension, which featured lightweight, cast aluminium alloy lower wishbones up front and cast semi-trailing arms at the rear. Like the new engine mountings, both items had originally been developed for the forthcoming 944 Turbo.

There is a price to pay for progress, of course, and in the case of the 944 it was an increase in price of DM 3600, taking the basic car to DM 48,950. Put another way, the 944 had gone up by more than 25% in just three years.

Across the Atlantic, on 31 August 1984, the long-running marketing agreement which resulted in Porsches and Audis being sold alongside each other under the auspices of Volkswagen of America Inc. finally came to an end. From now on, Porsche was on its own, with offices in Reno and the new distribution system utilizing 40 so-called 'Porsche Centres' across the US. Eventually, after a great deal of opposition from the existing dealers, this innovative plan was watered down somewhat, but amidst all the upheaval, American sales fell slightly in 1984, from 21,831 to 19,611 units. Incidentally, by far the best seller was the normally-aspirated 944, 13,036 of which found new homes in the States.

For 1985, the American's received a 32v five-litre version of the 928S, rated at 288bhp. By the summer of 1986, this model was offered in all markets, now known as the Series 4 and with a useful 320bhp on tap, giving the luxury GT a top speed of approaching 170mph.

Meanwhile, the 944 Turbo had been announced - a model covered in the next chapter - and sales picked up again. Indeed, another record was set in the process: 25,134 units for the year. The normally-aspirated 944 led the way, accounting for 15,395 units (or about 61% of total US sales), while the 944 Turbo found 1284 early buyers. The American market was now taking around 46% of Porsche production.

# 5
## ARRIVAL OF THE TURBO

In an owner's survey conducted by *Motor Trend* in 1984, when asked what they'd change about the 944, almost one-fifth of those interviewed would have liked more power, whilst a further 15% called for a turbo option. This was interesting, because one of the biggest problems - lack of steering wheel adjustment - was mentioned by less than 8% of those who answered the questionnaire. Obviously, the time was right to give the car a few more horses under the bonnet.

The first 944 model seen in public - the 1981 Le Mans racer - had been turbocharged, and almost exactly three years later, a prototype 944 Turbo had been entered in the annual 24-hour event held at Nelson Ledges in Ohio. Piloted by Freddy Baker, Jim Busby and Rick Knoop, it won the race easily (with a 40 lap margin over its nearest competitor, as it happens), so why was the 944 Turbo so long in coming? The official line cited uncertainty about the home market's future emissions laws, and the well-publicised German metalworker strike as reasons for the delay. However, in reality, there was little point in offering an even more attractive package when demand was still high for the normally-aspirated model.

As the months passed, though, Porsche could see that interest was tailing off, so rolled out its latest weapon in a bid to once again lengthen queues at dealerships. Enter the Type 951, better known as the 944 Turbo.

### The 944 Turbo
The new model received a number of subtle body modifications - a smooth, reinforced polyurethane nose section, minute sill extensions and a full-width spoiler underneath the rear bumper were the most obvious changes - primarily, in order to reduce drag and lift. However, the rear valance appendage also improved crosswind stability and transaxle cooling.

In addition to aerodynamic concerns, there were other reasons for the new front panel. As Tony Lapine said: "The shock-absorbing plastic nose section was technically and visually redesigned to provide optimal air inlets for charge-air cooling, engine cooling, oil cooling and ram-air cooling of the front brakes. In addition, high-beam headlights, fog lamps and parking lights are installed in the panel."

The windscreen, with the radio antenna embedded in the glass, was now bonded in place and the rain channels deleted to give smoother airflow over the body (both improvements were duly adopted on the normally-aspirated 944s for the 1986 model year, incidentally). The end result of all this fine tuning was a highly-efficient Cd of 0.33.

The interior was much like the latest 'oval dash' version on the normally-aspirated 944, except air conditioning came as standard, and the fuel economy gauge was replaced by a boost gauge. By far the biggest changes were to be found under the bonnet. As *Car & Driver* pointed out, Porsche "can legitimately lay claim to more turbocharging experience than any other manufacturer in the world." Not surprisingly, then, the

## What it takes to turbocharge a Porsche, including the turbocharger.

The theory that a whole is greater than the sum of its parts did not originate with Professor Porsche.

But he, for one, wholeheartedly subscribes to it.

Because if he's learned anything in four decades of building cars, it's that a change in one component can profoundly affect the performance of the others. And ultimately, the performance of the whole car.

Nowhere is this truth more evident than in the area of turbocharging.

Porsche pioneered this technology for production cars back in 1975. And realized right from the start that simply bolting on a turbocharger, tweaking the engine a little and re-naming the car was the wrong way to go about it.

The right way is revealed below.

Every component shown here was deemed necessary to transform a normally aspirated 944 into a turbocharged 944.

Major engine components, more than 30 in all, to compensate for increased internal loads and heat.

Chassis components, from shock absorbers and brakes to wheels and tires, to meet higher performance demands.

Front and rear body components, to improve wind resistance at higher speeds, while controlling lift and drag.

To say nothing of the turbocharger itself which, among other innovative bits of technology, includes two water cooling systems to protect turbine bearings, even after the engine is turned off.

Of course, if we hadn't gone to such lengths with the 944, we could still have built a turbo.

We just couldn't have built a Porsche.

*This superb advert from America shows all the major components used in converting the normally-aspirated 944 to a 944 Turbo. Although developed for the turbocharged model, a number of these parts, such as the cast aluminium alloy suspension pieces, were carried over onto the standard car.*

turbo installation in the 944 went a lot further than the typical bolt-on kit.

Although the basic construction and layout of the engine remained unchanged, in their quest for more power, Paul Hensler and his team of engineers added a KKK K26 turbocharger and specified new forged aluminium alloy pistons with recessed crowns, hollow-stemmed, sodium-filled exhaust valves, special ceramic liners in the exhaust ports, a beautifully-sculpted inlet manifold (to give equal length tracts to each cylinder), a different camshaft profile, a new oil pump, a separate oil cooler (to replace the oil-to-water heat exchanger found on normally-aspirated cars), and an air-to-air intercooler.

Unusually, the exhaust-driven turbocharger was positioned on the induction side of the powerplant. Although this complicated the unit's plumbing, it ultimately led to a number of advantages over traditional installations: there was a shorter distance between the turbo and intake manifold, meaning a significant reduction in turbo lag, and because of the long crossover pipe needed to join the exhaust on the opposite side of the engine, the air was much cooler by the time it entered the turbocharger. Interestingly, the entire exhaust system was constructed in heat-resistant steel tube, even the manifold, which was usually a much heavier cast-iron item. A further advantage was a better environment for the turbocharger. Turbos run hot anyway, but being mounted away from the heat of the exhaust helped keep it as cool as possible, thus improving long-term reliability. To further prolong the life of the turbocharger, it was given a separate thermostatically-controlled cooling system to dissipate heat from the vulnerable turbine bearings, even

89

*A pre-production version of the 944 Turbo. It took a keen eye to spot the differences between the standard 944 and its turbocharged stablemate, but, on closer examination, the smooth nose and rear underbody spoiler give the game away. The sill extensions, finished in black, were harder to spot.*

*Close-ups of the Turbo's elegant snout and rear underbody spoiler.*

after the engine was shut down (the first few minutes after a car is parked are critical moments regarding the longevity of a turbo).

The 944 Turbo was the first car in the world to offer the same power output from catalyst- and non-catalyst-equipped models - a remarkable achievement, and the initial step towards building Porsches with the same mechanical specification for all markets. Even with a three-way catalytic converter, the M44/51 engine produced 220bhp (or 217bhp in the US), thanks to the latest Bosch electronic anti-knock and boost-pressure control systems, and intensive charge air cooling.

Indeed, long-term development testing had shown the unit could remain reliable with 240bhp on tap, but 220bhp, developed at 5800rpm, represented a significant jump in power output and put a lot less stress on other components. Maximum torque was quoted as 243lbft at 3500rpm, and, courtesy of the fairly high 8.0:1 compression ratio, plenty of grunt was

*Interior of the Turbo, which was much the same as the normally-aspirated 944. This early car was trimmed in the attractive 'Porsche' fabric*

*The 944 Turbo engine. Note the blower in the centre of the picture, and the long crossover pipe running around the back of the power unit.*

available from low revs - something lacking in the majority of turbocharged road cars. At the other end of the rev band, 11psi of maximum turbo boost provided sparkling overtaking performance.

Uprated engine mountings were employed, not to deal with the additional weight (amazingly, it was only 35lbs, or 15.9kg, heavier than the standard 944 unit), but the extra heat from the turbocharger. These were also used on the normally-aspirated model, as extreme temperatures had caused problems on earlier cars, while the aluminium sump shield was modified to direct additional cooling air towards them, reduce heat build-up around the power unit, and smooth airflow underneath the vehicle.

The five-speed gearbox was new - designated type 083D - with gear ratios quite different to those of the normally-aspirated car; namely 3.50:1 on first, 2.06 on second, 1.40 on third, an almost direct 1.03 on fourth, and 0.83:1 on top. In addition, a beefier 240mm (9.4in) clutch, transmission cooler and higher 3.38:1 final-drive ratio were employed; a limited-slip differential was optional. An automatic 'box was not available.

Naturally, the new light alloy suspension parts described in the last chapter were specified, along with stiffer spring rates and uprated gas-filled shock absorbers. Anti-roll bars were fitted at the front and rear, 22.5 and 18mm in diameter, respectively (0.88 and 0.71in). A further uprated Sport suspension, with Koni adjustable shock absorbers, was available as an option.

Meanwhile, larger diameter discs (297mm up front, 300 at the rear, or 11.7 and 11.8in respectively) and four-piston, aluminium alloy brake calipers (made by the famous Brembo concern) were adopted for greater heat dissipation and stopping power.

*The turbocharged engine was a tight fit in the 944. Note the hydraulic struts on the bonnet, helping to raise the panel and keep it in place until ready to be closed again. These were fitted to the 944 from inception, whilst the cheaper 924 employed a simple steel rod as a prop. Lighting was provided in both the engine bay and luggage compartment.*

Power-assisted steering came as part of the package, combined with a leather-trimmed 360mm (14.17in) diameter four-spoke steering wheel. Cast 7J x 16 alloys at the front (shod with 205/55 VR-rated rubber) and 8J x 16 items at the rear with wider 225/50 tyres were standard fare, with 16-inch, five-spoke forged alloy wheels (also with 7 and 8J rim widths) optional.

In Europe, a typical car weighed in at 2975lbs (1349kg), or about 200lbs (90kg) more than a contemporary, normally-aspirated model (weight distribution was exactly 50/50 over the two axles). According to Porsche, the Turbo was capable of 152mph (243kph) and covering the 0-60 yardstick in 6.3 seconds - remember, factory figures have always been conservative!

A total of 15 prototypes had been built in anticipation of the car's introduction to the press in the south of France during February 1985, followed by a further 100 pre-production models shortly after this date. By July, when

*As with all of Porsche's water-cooled models, the transaxle arrangement was retained for the Turbo. The wheels were the same design as those found on the normally-aspirated 944, but a bigger size.*

*An early press picture of the new 944 Turbo. The redesigned nose section certainly gave the car a purposeful look.*

*Rear three-quarter view of the Turbo. It was earmarked as a replacement for the 911 at one stage - once more though, the evergreen rear-engined model survived to tell the tale. The rear underbody spoiler is easy to see in this shot.*

*Although the steering wheel remained fixed, the seat height was adjustable. Three types of seat were available on the Turbo, incidentally - standard, sport or luxury. Note the boost gauge underneath the tachometer.*

*Tail of the 944 Turbo. Note the 'turbo' script where the '944' badge usually appears, and the 'Porsche' insignia stamped into the rear spoiler.*

the 944 Turbo went on sale to the public, the Neckarsulm works was building a total of 150 four-cylinder Porsches a day, the vast majority of them 944s.

The 944 Turbo certainly wasn't cheap at DM 74,000 (or DM 21,750 more than the standard 944). The turbocharged model was expected to reach British showrooms in November, priced at around £27,000. At this price, Porsche GB felt it could sell around 200 Turbos a year in the UK. In the end, the model was announced at £25,312 (although equipped with air conditioning, a sunroof, power leather trimmed seats with cloth inlays, headlight washers, electric windows and door mirrors, a Panasonic four-speaker stereo radio/cassette and central locking as standard, it was hard to disguise the fact that it was only £10 shy of the price of a 911 Carrera), before receiving a hefty £2235 increase shortly after.

However, a wave of enthusiasm from the motoring press meant that sales didn't seem to suffer, despite the fact that a Jaguar XJ-S HE, a BMW 635CSi or a classic Mercedes 380SL could be bought for similar money, or maybe a Lamborghini Jalpa or Ferrari 308GTB qv for just a little more.

### Early press reaction

At the time of the press launch, Peter Schutz said: "It's the first of a new breed of Porsche, giving the sporting driver more comfort, and providing the comfort driver with more performance." Judging by contemporary press reaction, Schutz could be rightfully proud of this latest addition to the range, as the model fully upheld the Stuttgart marque's slogan of 'Driving in its Finest Form'.

In the March 1985 issue of *MotorSport*, after concluding that the

*Press pictures released by Porsche Cars GB showing "The new Porsche 944 Turbo." The number plate was very apt, and, not surprisingly, was transferred to a number of 944s over the years.*

*The 1986 944 Turbo with optional 16-inch Fuchs forged alloys finished with matching centres.*

*A German-registered 944 Turbo. The Turbo was ideally suited to road conditions in Germany, where it was possible to cruise at high speed from one end of the country to the other.*

Turbo was as quick as a 911 Carrera, it said: "What is remarkable about this sports car is that the turbocharger is completely unobtrusive, with massive power and torque distributed throughout the range, so that it comes as a surprise to see the maximum speed of 153mph (245kph) indicated on the speedometer within seconds of a clear stretch of road presenting itself!

"Even allowing for a 5% speedometer error, which the engineers admitted as a possibility, the performance was nothing less than amazing since the engine noise remained subdued, and the most obvious sounds were the rustle of wind around the door mirror and the thump of wide tyres over road joints. It is utterly unlike the 911 which is a more bustling, vivacious car altogether."

*Motor* magazine said: "It would be hard to imagine power steering any better than this car's. The assistance plays a supporting role to response, accuracy and informative feedback - as it should do - but the driver needs to exert no great effort at the helm when parking. In fact it's a sense of effortlessness and calm control that the driver is most aware of when conducting the car briskly, too. There's masses of grip and quick, accurately obedient turn-in to rely on at all times and, in most circumstances, the rear tyres stick to the tarmac like marmalade to a blanket."

The *Autocar* found that "Handling remains beautifully neutral with subjectively less understeer than the standard 944 Lux. With 220bhp on tap, despite the wider 225-section rear tyres, it is possible to generate an oversteering tail-slide, but such is the car's inherent grip and balance that the slide remains supremely controllable on the throttle, an organ-type pedal which, thanks to its long travel, permits the driver to make very fine corrections. In short, the 944 Turbo is a car which flatters the driver, allowing him an exuberant driving style - if he chooses - in perfect safety.

*For those not satisfied with the standard Turbo, there were plenty of aftermarket tuners who were only too happy to 'modify' it. This advert is from the famous Strosek concern in Germany.*

The US spec 944 Turbo at the time of its launch. To comply with North American regulations, side markers had to be incorporated into the new nose panel; the rear ones remained in the original spot, situated between the rear wheelarch and the bumper.

Interior of the US Turbo model. Note the seat adjustment switches and leather trim.

"The other side of the coin is, of course, ride quality, and this is where a toll is extracted for the excellent handling of the chassis. Undoubtedly the ride on marble-smooth German *autobahnen* would be quite acceptable for a sports coupé. Introduce the 944 Turbo to the badly-surfaced roads of Britain, as well as those of some Continental countries, and the ride becomes decidedly busy, exhibiting a distinctly harsh reaction to certain sharp-edged surface irregularities along with strong bump-thump.

"By comparison, the standard fitment power-assisted rack and pinion steering, with its 3.2 turns lock-to-lock, is an absolute joy ... We were able to record an overall consumption figure of 22.9mpg for our hard-driven test car, a figure which, it should be pointed out, is only 1.8mpg worse than that of the recently tested Porsche 944 Lux."

The testers appreciated the seats, with adjustment in three directions and optional heating (available for £234), and the new dashboard, although the steering wheel obstructed the view of some of the gauges. Having recorded a one-way best of 158mph (253kph) and a 14.8 second standing-quarter, the verdict was hardly surprising - "Porsche has created another winner."

Writing for *Classic Cars*, Tony Dron, who had campaigned the 924 Carrera GT at Le Mans, noted: "Top speed is all very well but it is meaningless on its own. In some cars, the noise at high speeds is unbearable, the lack of stability leads to white-knuckle motoring in a straight line, and all the while the driver is studying the instruments to look for signs of rising temperatures and falling oil pressure. No such problems afflict the 944 Turbo. It has a strong heart ...

"With the 944 Turbo you can enjoy the performance properly as the steering feels magnificent at all speeds and the carefully thought out suspension and aerodynamics combine to give the driver complete confidence in the stability of the car, and thus his own ability to control it safely.

"Throughout the speed range, the 944 Turbo has a magnificent ride and there is something about the car's handling, beyond technical description, that makes it feel willing to accept changes in direction and high cornering forces without drama. This 'feel' is hard to define but it is an undeniable pleasure to experience. In short, the 944 Turbo is capable of delivering the sports car performance that any owner would be hoping for.

"How about fuel consumption? I got 24.0mpg over 892 miles, which is remarkably good. It would be easy to achieve 30mpg giving a range of around 420-530 miles between fuel stops. Though the 944 Turbo did not have ABS brakes, the braking system on the car is excellent and well up to the severe demands placed on it by the stunning performance."

There were areas in which the Turbo slipped up, but they were few and far between. Although generally impressed with the engine, which was described as "a technical tour de force," *What Car?* felt "there has been a slight loss in smoothness, however: gone is the fabulously silky feel that made the standard 944 so remarkable for a big four-cylinder machine. Many, too, will regret the absence of the flat-six's searing scream as the revs rush round the dial."

The *Autocar* adored the Turbo's performance and handling, but cited the gearchange and amount of road noise as areas not in keeping with the rest of the car's qualities. Some other testers commented on the sill extensions grounding on occasion, but in reality it is doubtful whether the average owner would ever experience this particular problem.

## The Turbo in America

With LE-Jetronic fuel-injection, instead of L-Jetronic, but the same 8.0:1 compression ratio as European models, the US spec engine produced 217bhp at 5800rpm (the red-line was marked at 6400rpm, 100rpm below the electronic fuel cut-off) and 243lbft at 3500rpm. In the States, this represented a 52% increase in power and a truly massive 77% gain in torque over the original 944.

It was fitted with the same five-speed manual gearbox and final-drive as European models, as well as the same wheels and tyres. Thus, according to official figures released in the States, the 0-60 time went down from 8.3 to 6.1 seconds, whilst the standing-quarter was covered in 14.4 seconds - an improvement of 1.8 seconds. At the same time, top speed increased from 131 (210) to 152mph (243kph).

944 Turbos headed for America came with automatic air conditioning,

## By the time anyone begins to catch up, we will have moved ahead again.

The success of the 928S proved that there was, indeed, more than one "right" way to build a Porsche.

It also set the stage for the next important step in the evolution of the sports car as defined by Porsche.

The 944.

A car designed to benefit not only from the very latest technology, but from everything four decades of building and racing sports cars had taught us.

A car in which more people than ever before would be able to experience the sheer exhilaration of driving a Porsche.

From the beginning, the 944 was an unqualified success.

Car and Driver Magazine voted it "One of the Ten Best Cars in America" for four years running. And last year, declared it "The Best Handling Production Sports Car in America."

But, more important, people bought

*Early American advertising for the 944 Turbo. For anoraks, the 16-inch alloy wheels - a standard fitment on the turbocharged model - could be distinguished from the 15-inch items by the deeper design at the rear, and the extra distance between the 'Telephone Dial' and the rim.*

ved sports cars. And never owned one before. orsche hasn't led its after year by resting on this year is no different. r you see here. 944 Turbo. mance of the 944 can xhilarating, the per- machine almost defies ause we were able to wer by a staggering 50% in a four-cylinder engine that was already one of the biggest, most powerful fours in production.

But because we didn't leave it at that. Professor Porsche's philosophy simply doesn't allow for bolting on a turbocharger and renaming the car.

Every element of the 944 Turbo—engine, transaxle, suspension, brakes, tires, aerodynamics—was re-thought and re-engineered to meet the most demanding criteria for performance and handling.

The result, for you, is a brand-new car. And for our competition, a brand-new goal.

**944 Turbo** *4-cylinder, in-line, single overhead camshaft, liquid-cooled, front engine with turbocharger and intercooler, 2479cc, 217 hp., transaxle. Weight: 2899 lbs. Top Speed: 152 mph.*

an electrically-adjustable driver's seat, and electric windows and door mirrors. Popular options included a stereo radio/cassette ($625) and an electric sunroof (listed at $695), which naturally was added to the introductory $29,500 base price.

The low sticker price was extremely competitive, prompting the US press to fall head over heels in love with the Turbo. When *Road & Track* brought the Porsche 944, 944 Turbo, 911 Cabriolet, 911 Turbo and 928S together, it concluded: "These are five very different cars. They are different on purpose, because Porsche intended for them each to do different things well.

"If there's a winner, it's one based on value. The 944 Turbo delivers more road performance and loses less in driveability or at monthly payment time than the others."

With the 911 Turbo at $48,000 and the 928S $2000 more than that, when one adds in the fact that the 944 Turbo had the highest top speed, economy figures only the normally-aspirated 944 could beat, and by far the best showing on the skidpan, it's easy to see why the magazine reached this conclusion.

The same journal later compared the 944 Turbo with the Chevrolet Corvette and Mazda RX-7 Turbo. While the rotary-engined car was not as quick as the other two, and not quite as handy around the skidpan, there was little to separate them on paper. At the end of the test, the German machine won all three categories - Performance, Comfort/Controls and Design/Styling

*Spy shots taken during the early part of 1985 suggested the possibility of a 944 Targa, although those with sources close to the factory were predicting that a full drophead coupé would be introduced in the near future. Sure enough, this prototype made a surprise appearance at the 1985 Frankfurt Show.*

*Another view of the prototype convertible displayed at the Frankfurt Show, this time with the hood in the raised position.*

- finishing with 76 points against 70 for the 'Vette and 67 for the RX.

In the following month, *Road & Track* tracked the route of the Mille Miglia in a 944 Turbo, an Alfa GTV6, a Corvette, Jaguar XJ-SC HE and Nissan 300ZX Turbo. The 944 was declared the car the testers, including ex-F1 maestro, Phil Hill, would most like to pick for their touring holiday. They said: "The Porsche simply did everything well and was a pleasure to drive. Period."

Incidentally, after the first 400 or so cars were built, all further 944s supplied for the North American market were fitted with a third high-level brake light in order to comply with the latest batch of Federal regulations.

## 944 update

At the 1985 Frankfurt Show, naturally enough the recently-introduced 944 Turbo was given pride of place on the Porsche stand, but it was a prototype convertible that stole the limelight, put there to gauge customer reaction. It was powered by the forthcoming 16v engine and featured an electrically-operated hood. Crowds surrounded the machine throughout the event, so it was perhaps inevitable that one day a soft-top 944 would join the range - early predictions in the motoring press favoured a 1988 introduction.

Like the Turbo, the 1986 MY normally-aspirated 944 was also equipped with a stainless steel exhaust manifold and, for the home market, a

*The 944 for the 1986 model year.*

> **Standard coachwork colours (1986 MY)**
> Black, Pastel Beige, Guards Red, Copenhagen Blue, Alpine White.
>
> **Special coachwork colours**
> Graphite Metallic, Garnet Red Metallic, Kalahari Metallic, Stone Grey Metallic, Crystal Green Metallic, Sapphire Metallic, Mahogany Metallic, Zermatt Silver Metallic.
>
> **Trim materials**
> Black, brown or light grey leatherette with matching inlays. Alternatively, inlays could be in pinstripe velour (black with white, brown with beige or light grey with white); seat facings could also be supplied in pinstripe flannel cloth (in the same shades as the velour inlays), black, brown or light grey 'Porsche' cloth or leather as an option. Carpets came in black, brown, burgundy or light grey.

catalytic converter in preparation for Germany's new regulations. The latter prompted Porsche to cancel all further development work on engines designed to run on leaded fuel, and gave added impetus to introduce catalyst-equipped power units suitable for all markets.

In the United States, a hike in the compression ratio from 9.5 to 9.7:1 (brought about by the new pistons mentioned in chapter four) saw a small gain in power output - up 4bhp to 147 at 5800rpm - and torque, now quoted at 140lbft at 3000rpm.

With the same gearing as before, the $22,950 944 was compared with the latest Mazda RX-7 in the February 1986 issue of Road & Track. Although the Japanese car was both cheaper and better equipped - options for the Stuttgart machine included a $2715 Touring Package, 15-inch Fuchs alloys ($744), a limited-slip differential ($595), uprated suspension ($295), central locking ($250), a stereo radio/cassette ($625) and sports seats ($590) - the article ended with the following words: "The 944 is still the better sports/GT car, and Porsche continues to pay what Cadillac used to call the penalty of leadership, i.e. the 944 is still the target."

By the end of 1985, reports were starting to circulate of braking problems with the 944 and 928 . Several cars in Europe had apparently developed a noticeable judder, though

*A 1986 944 pictured in perfect Porsche country. American spec cars now had 147bhp and 140lbft of torque.*

there was no such problem in the States, possibly due to the different pad materials used in the two markets, and the USA's lower average speeds.

The British magazine, *Performance Car*, tried the latest 944 and recorded a 0-60 time of 7.6 seconds, and a 15.7 second standing-quarter; overall fuel consumption was a very reasonable 26.2mpg. In 11 catagories, the Porsche rated four out of five stars in nine of them - Engine, Gearchange (although a vibration through the lever was noted, something familiar to a lot of 924 owners), Gear Ratios, Clutch, Handling, Roadholding, Comfort,

*One of a series of publicity pictures taken for the 924/944 series catalogue. The same photographs continued to appear for several years.*

*Another shot taken from the batch of brochure pictures. The 944 looked superb in the darker metallic colours.*

Interior and Overall Enjoyment - while the brakes got full marks; the ride was the only let down, with three out of five marks.

Meanwhile, though, the competition was catching up fast. In the UK, the Mitsubishi Starion (which should have been Stallion, by the way!) was only £1000 or so different in price to the 944 back in 1982, so, with the two being so similarly priced, most of the previous road tests were in favour of the Stuttgart machine due to its superior pedigree. However, following a spate of price increases in Germany, by 1986 there was a much bigger difference: the Porsche cost £18,234 compared to £13,549 for the Japanese car; a

*A German registered 944. From 1986, the body carried a ten year anti-perforation warranty, whilst cars for the home market were fitted with a catalytic converter.*

big enough gap to make most people rethink the equation.

Following a comparison of the two vehicles, *Fast Lane* eventually concluded: "The Starion makes an impressive case for itself. It's fast - a touch faster than the 944 in fact - and has a devastating turn of speed when the turbo is in full cry ... Dynamically, the Porsche is still the better car ... The Porsche also exudes charisma ... It's a high price to pay for something so indefinable but then exclusivity is presumably part of the appeal, too. If you can't afford it, never mind. Go for the Starion and think of the money you're saving."

Power-assisted steering, a headlight washer system, four-

> *British advertising for the 944. As 1986 drew to a close, Porsche GB revealed that 6014 944s had been sold in the UK since its introduction. Of this figure, 754 were automatics and 353 were turbocharged.*

speaker Panasonic radio/cassette, electric windows and door mirrors, and a rear wiper came as standard, but the option list was still lengthy. Popular extras included the 16-inch forged alloys (£1436), a limited-slip differential (£529), air conditioning (£1187), leather trim (£1279), a sunroof (£703), central locking (£238), front fog lights (£142), and a cassette/coin holder at £64.

## The fate of the 924

The Stuttgart company was faced with two major problems as it entered the mid-1980s: the short supply of Audi-built powerplants and Germany's latest emissions regulations. The new guidelines went into force in January 1986, stipulating a requirement for all new vehicles to use three-way catalytic converters in order to avoid a hefty pollution tax.

It was an interesting development, but the lack of unleaded fuel in other parts of Europe made rather a mockery of it, and it was no mere coincidence that the basic price of a 944 in Germany rose by 7% after being equipped with a 'cat'. However, with so many cars staying in Germany for home market consumption, the catalytic converter issue was just as important to Porsche as changes in Federal requirements for the majority of sports car manufacturers.

It had been speculated for some time that the 924 would continue in one form or another, some suggesting that it would be powered by a two-litre version of the 944 engine, others predicting the possibility of another Audi-based unit, perhaps even the fuel-injected 2.1 litre five-cylinder powerplant. In the end, Porsche decided to keep the 944 lump as it was, albeit with a few minor modifications.

Overnight, this gave the 924 a new lease of life and silenced the model's critics in one blow, but there was still a problem. The 924 was both lighter and cleaner through the air than a 944, so with the same power the 924 would have been faster than its more expensive stablemate, and that simply couldn't be allowed to happen. For that reason, power was reduced slightly in order to keep the 944 ahead in the performance stakes. As a matter of interest, due to a lower 9.7:1 compression ratio, the 924S - as the new model was known - came with 150bhp and 144lbft of torque.

Introduced in Germany at DM 41,950 (which represented a massive 21% increase over the outgoing two-litre 924), its Frankfurt Show debut was somewhat overshadowed by the recently-introduced 944 Turbo and the surprise appearance of the 944

*Powered by a detuned version of the 944 engine, the 924S replaced the old two-litre 924. The body remained largely unchanged, except for the lack of rain channels (something introduced on all 1986 four-cylinder models), and different badging; the dashboard and interior were carried over from the 924. The attractive cast alloys looked similar to the 944 items, but had narrower 6J rims shod with 195/65 VR15 rubber.*

Cabriolet prototype. Although it would be some time before the latter went into production, there's no doubt that it stole a lot of the thunder. The timing could have been better in other ways, too, as in mid-1985, Volkswagen had launched the 16v version of the Scirocco GTi. With 139bhp on tap in a lighter body, performance was easily on a par with the Porsche newcomer but, on the UK market, for instance, it cost a substantial 35% less than the basic 924S.

The only saving grace, as far as performance car makers were concerned, was that oil prices plummeted in 1986. Cheaper oil equals cheaper petrol, which tends to boost sales of larger-engined machines.

## The Turbo Cup

1986 saw the introduction of the factory-run Porsche Turbo Cup racing series. Initially a seven-race domestic programme was established using near-standard 944 Turbos (the only real modifications were a stripped out interior and a rollcage, although they were some 155lbs - or 70kg - lighter than the standard road version); 40 cars were built for the event, costing no less than DM 78,900 each.

The Turbo Cup proved extremely popular, with Joachim Winkelhock winning the first series. For 1987 the 944 racers were given 250bhp and a number of chassis modifications, including stiffer anti-roll bars and springs, uprated shock absorbers and ABS braking. Deleting the sunroof, air conditioning, electric windows and underseal resulted in these new

*The Porsche range for the 1986 model year. Of the four-cylinder cars, the standard 944 can be seen on the left (for some strange reason, with US spec rear bumpers, although the rest of the vehicle complies with European regulations), with the 944 Turbo behind it; at the back we have the 924S. The other models include the 911 Turbo, 911 Carrera Cabriolet and the 928S.*

*One of 40 cars built for the Porsche Turbo Cup race series.*

*Rear view of the same car, looking very purposeful with the wide rubber at the rear. The batch of Turbo Cup racers was completed in March 1986.*

*A Turbo Cup racer prepared for battle.*

*The Turbo Cup racing series was introduced in 1986, initially taking in seven rounds held in Germany. This picture shows Uwe Eickwinkel leading a gaggle of 944s at Hockenheim in June.*

models - now costing a hefty DM 95,000 - being the same weight as the 1986 cars. With the extra power on tap, they were capable of over 160mph.

In addition, the championship rounds spread across Europe, taking in Monza, Jarama, Brünn (Brno), the Salzburgring and Spa, as well as German tracks, while Sonauto sponsored its own series in France: later, Canada also had a version of the Turbo Cup.

I don't wish to dwell on this element of the car's racing history, as I don't consider a one-make series an historically significant form of competition as far as a vehicle is concerned; after all, it's obvious which make and model is going to win, so it is more a test of the drivers. Suffice to say that, after three years with the 250bhp 944 Turbo, in 1990, the Turbo Cup became the Carrera Cup, following the move to 911s for the series, before ultimately being christened the Porsche Supercup in 1993.

Perhaps the biggest advantage of the Turbo Cup was the publicity the championship brought the Stuttgart company, and the ultimate development of the equivalent 250bhp road car.

## The 944S

In the November 1985 issue of *Road & Track*, John Dinkel wrote: "[The 928] recently received a four-valve version of its 4.7 litre V8. If you remember that the 944 engine is basically half that V8, then it doesn't take a genius to figure out that a 944S has got to be right around the corner. The four-valve 944S will put out about 180bhp compared with 143 for the current normally-aspirated 944. Naturally, the 944 Turbo will get the four-valve head, again with a commensurate increase in performance from its current 220bhp up to what I'd estimate would be 250-260."

It was a good prediction, even down to the name. Of course, the 1981 Le Mans car had sported a 16v head, but it was the 928 that received it first - or rather, two of them, one for each bank of the mighty V8 - following the introduction of the 32v five-litre 928S. With the 924S now offering similar performance to the more expensive 944, it was only a matter of time before a faster normally-aspirated version of the latter reached the market. The 16v

*Head-on view of the 944S engine, the 16v unit being announced in June 1986, although the official launch of the new car was at the Frankfurt Show three months later.*

head provided the obvious answer.

The necessary modifications were kept to a minimum. The basic construction was very much the same as that for the standard 944, but, naturally, being a 16v head, each cylinder was given two inlet and two exhaust valves rather than one, with the single sparkplug situated in the centre of the pent-roof combustion

*The 16v cylinder head. The exhaust camshaft, driven by the crankshaft via toothed belt, was used to drive the inlet cam by the central chain. The latter can be seen clearly in this picture.*

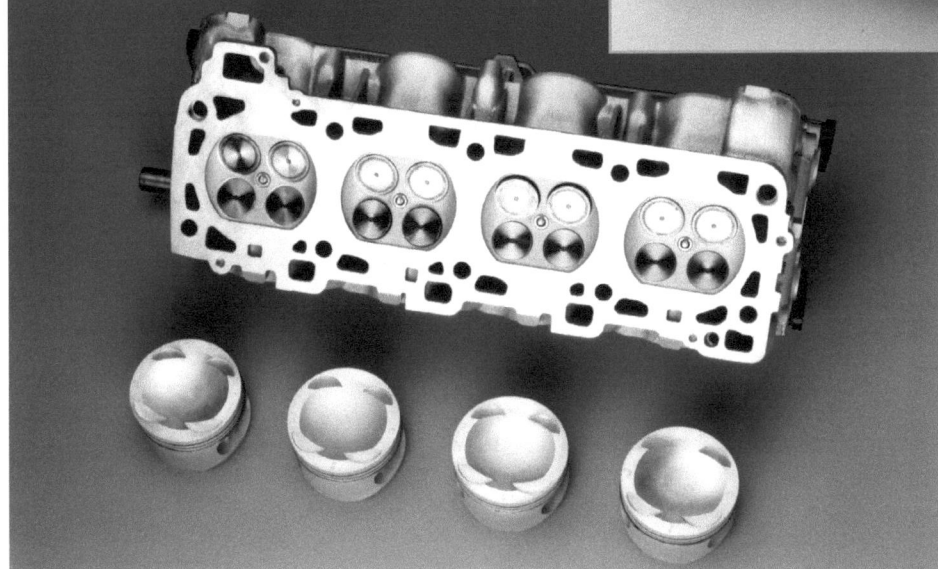

chamber. The Bosch L-Jetronic fuel-injection was retained.

To operate the valves (at 35mm, or 1.38in, they were slightly smaller in diameter than those found in the 8v powerplant), the 16-valve engine used twin cams instead of one, although the

*The other side of the head. The four valves per cylinder and combustion chamber shape combined with a central sparkplug helped the engine at higher revs, but some complained of the subsequent loss of low-end torque. The recessed crowns in the pistons are also shown here.*

*The 16v unit installed in the 944 engine bay.*

new exhaust camshaft was located in the same place as the single original item, as it was this that drove the inlet camshaft via a hydraulically-tensioned central chain. Like the 944 unit, initial drive from the crankshaft was transmitted by a toothed belt, wider and stronger than before and kept taut by a redesigned tensioner.

For better breathing, the head had wider intake and exhaust ports than those found on the V8, so the manifolds were given larger internal bores to suit. This was one of the few changes specified for the four-cylinder head, but it was easily achieved and resulted in a high-revving engine with a 6800rpm red-line. By the way,

*A press release picture from when the car was announced, this particular example sporting the optional 16-inch alloy wheels. Note the small '16 Ventiler' badge beyond the repeater indicator on the front wing.*

assembly of the 16v head was carried out by robots - a far cry from Porsche's early days in Gmünd.

With the same bore and stroke as the other 944 models, the 2479cc capacity was retained, but thanks to the new head and a 10.9:1 compression ratio (knock sensors from the Turbo

*Interior of the 944S, which was much the same as that of the standard 944.*

*Rear three-quarter view of the same car. Not surprisingly, the 944S had only been launched five minutes before elements of the press were wondering when the 16v Turbo would arrive!*

were responsible for allowing this high c/r in all markets), the M44/40 unit developed a healthy 190bhp at 6000rpm and 170lbft of torque at 4300 - enough to take the S to a top speed of 142mph (227kph). Being a 'world' engine, the addition of a catalytic converter failed to blunt its performance, so cars supplied to North America were endowed with a near-identical 188bhp and 170lbft at the same revs.

All markets received the Turbo's transmission, combined with the 944's 3.89:1 final-drive ratio, giving intermediate speeds of 36, 61, 90 and 123mph (58, 98, 144 and 197kph, respectively). As with the turbocharged car, an automatic gearbox was not available.

The suspension was sourced from the 944, albeit with subtly revised geometry; anti-roll bars were fitted front and rear on European models, but at the front only for cars headed Stateside (a rear bar could be bought separately, if required).

Likewise, brakes were carried over from the normally-aspirated model, as were the standard alloys - 'telephone dial' 7J x 15 cast items, which came shod with 195/65 VR-rated tyres, or 215/60s for the American market. Incidentally, the normal US spec 944 continued to use this wider rubber, presumably for appearance's sake in view of the low national speed limit.

Returning to the S, ABS braking was optional, along with a limited-slip differential, stiffer Sport suspension and 928-type 16-inch disc-style forged alloys. For serious enthusiasts, there was also a Club Sport/Performance Handling Package (also available for the Turbo), which converted a road car into one suitable for the race track.

Bodily, there was little difference between the 944 and the 944S. The new arrival gained a colour-keyed '16 Ventiler' badge on the front wing, which merged nicely with the rubbing strips when fitted, and '944S' script on the tail. Otherwise the two models looked the same from the outside.

It was a similar story inside. Power-assisted steering, electrically-adjustable door mirrors, central locking, headlight washers, rear wash/wipe, tinted glass and a stereo radio/cassette came as standard in Europe, but the option list remained lengthy. Apart from the mechanical items, metallic paint, a sunroof, front fog lights, leather trim, a graduated front windscreen, a cassette/coin holder, even cloth door trim panels and cloth seat bolsters, remained cost extras. Americans had to fork out for a stereo, but PCNA offered a Touring Package that included a sunroof, cruise control, a rear wiper, leather trim, a leather-covered steering wheel, and an alarm.

The only advantage for the sporting driver was that, combined with the use of magnesium alloys for some of the unique engine components, the basic S weighed only 22lbs (10kg) more than the standard 944. Always look on the bright side of life ...

Introduced at the 1986 Frankfurt Show, the 16v model slotted in neatly between the existing 944 and the Turbo, priced at DM 61,355 - about DM 6000 more than the former and DM 16,000 less than the latter. When the 944S duly reached export markets, this translated to $28,250 in the States and £25,303 in the UK (£1306 more than at the time of its announcement, and adding leather trim and a sunroof soon took it towards £28,000).

## Some thoughts on the 944S

Writing for *Car & Driver*, Arthur St Antoine felt "The power delivery in

*Regarding the 944S, road test reactions were mixed to say the least. Conditions in which to enjoy the 16v unit to the full were becoming increasingly rare in Europe, and virtually non-existent in America without attracting the attention of the law. This led many to question the model's worth.*

*The colour-keyed '16 Ventiler' badge was even more discreet when side-rubbing strips were specified (standard in the UK). Without looking carefully at the front wing, when equipped with the standard alloys (seen here), it was necessary to see the tail or open the bonnet in order to distinguish the 944S from its cheaper stablemate.*

*A final view of the 944S for the time being - a German registered 1987 model with optional disc-type forged alloy wheels. The factory used this car in a number of publicity shots.*

the 944S is wonderfully smooth and consistent - certainly better than that of the current 944 Turbo. Which makes the 944S just about my favourite Porsche. Until, of course, the 944S Turbo comes along."

Having clocked a highly creditable 6.8 second 0-60mph time and a 15.2 second standing-quarter, his colleague, Larry Griffin, was also generally impressed, particularly with the steering: "The exceptional feel through the power steering and the leather-wrapped wheel provides a most direct link with the world stroking past the windows." He added: "The base seats are good and their power height adjustments are handy, but the sport-seat option, packed with the best bolstering Recaro builds at a reasonable price, is unsurpassed for athletic support." These could be bought either as a pair or for the driver only, incidentally.

But it wasn't all good news. In England, *MotorSport* magazine noted: "Possibly one is looking for extraordinary performance, and a claimed top speed of 142mph is impressive, but few of us stray into that area on British roads unless we want to lose our licences. The claimed 0-62mph time of 7.9 seconds is respectable, but there are currently 'hot hatches' which will beat it.

"One cannot even say that the car's overall feel is exceptional. There's nothing wrong with it, it's taut and competent, it has a pleasant ride, noise levels are low (save for the boom from the rear suspension when going over bumps) but at the price one expects something extraordinary."

Following the full road test, the same journal praised the "outstanding handling" and "free-revving engine," but made the comment: "It is easy to say that the 944 Lux represents better value for money, but that is hardly a criticism of the new S. Perhaps in 'fine tuning' the specification of its range, the German company should consider fine tuning its price structure as well. The critics are right. Objectively, the 944S is a fine car, but its biggest competitor comes from within Porsche's own ranks." With Porsche hoping that the S would account for more than half of the normally-aspirated 944 sales in the UK, this was not a good sign.

*Motor* also had doubts about the new package: "According to Porsche's published torque curves, the 944S should match the identically geared 944 Lux for low- and mid-range lugging power. In practice, the results are rather different, the 16-valve car taking 7.4 seconds to cover the 30-50mph increment in fourth (6.2 seconds for the Lux) and 8.8 seconds to cover 50-70mph in fifth (against 8.4 seconds). As this progression suggests, the 944S turns the tables on the Lux in the higher speed ranges - its fifth gear 80-100mph time of 9.6 seconds handsomely beats the 11.4 of the Lux.

"The wonderfully deep-chested shove from low revs of the eight-valve car just never materialises. What mid-range punch there is feels soft-edged, cushioned, unexciting. The engine never appears weak-kneed, but neither does it ever recreate the sense of effortlessness so endearing in its

> **Standard coachwork colours (1987 MY)**
> Black, Summer Yellow, Guards Red, Crimson Red, Azure Blue, Alpine White.
>
> **Special coachwork colours**
> Nougat Brown Metallic, Flamingo Metallic, Diamond Blue Metallic, Maraschino Red Metallic, Almond Metallic, Satin Black Metallic, Nile Green Metallic, Ocean Blue Metallic, Stone Grey Metallic, Zermatt Silver Metallic.
>
> **Trim materials**
> Black, brown, burgundy or light grey leatherette with matching inlays. Alternatively, inlays could be in pinstripe velour (black with white, brown with beige, burgundy with white or light grey with white); seat facings could also be supplied in pinstripe flannel cloth (in the same shades as the velour inlays), black, brown, burgundy or light grey 'Porsche' cloth or leather as an option. Carpets came in black, brown, burgundy or light grey.

more simply engineered stablemate. That said, the engine's top end urge is a source of satisfaction.

"The 944's gearchange is so good, you'd never suspect the existence of the long linkage involved in its transaxle layout. Its action is meaty yet beautifully precise and smooth, its engineering quality tactile, rewarding. The clutch, too, has a friendly, well-cushioned action.

"The 944S returned 21.9mpg overall, which must be judged disappointing in the light of the 24.8mpg we recorded for the 944 Lux, though it can't be all that surprising for an engine so frenetic in nature."

From this, we can establish several plus and minus points. Increased performance over the standard 944 was evident, sure enough, but only at far higher revs (from 4000rpm onwards), and then at the expense of fuel consumption and initial outlay. In terms of sales, this lack of a definite benefit for the extra money asked would cost Porsche dearly in the future, especially in the American market where the price difference between the S and the Turbo was only a measly $5000.

The competition was strong in this sector, too. The Nissan 300ZX Turbo, facelifted for 1987, offered slightly better straight-line performance and a high standard specification for £5000 less, whilst the Lotus Excel SE was cheaper still. Then, of course, there was the Ford Sierra RS Cosworth, which was both substantially quicker and passed on a £7500 saving, or, for those who wanted something a little more exclusive, the glamorous Renault GTA Turbo.

When *What Car?* compared the 944S and the new Renault in early 1987, it stated that the Porsche had the better ride and handling, but that the French car had the upper hand in the performance stakes. Otherwise, it was neck and neck throughout the test. It concluded: "The 944S is the safe, sensible choice, the Renault Turbo a riskier proposition that's excitingly different."

## Other 1987 model year news

For 1987, 944s - and indeed 924Ss - had a new timing belt pre-tensioner (borrowed from the V8 unit) fitted to reduce maintenance. The 944 also received an improved limited-slip differential (when specified), a pressure limiting valve for the rear brakes, and uprated driveshafts. Wider Turbo wheels and tyres became optional, along with the 16-inch forged disc-type alloys. Other options included a ten-speaker audio system and split rear seats. This latter feature was useful but meant losing the roller-blind luggage cover, which was replaced by a rather flimsier, curtain-type item.

In the UK, the basic 1987 model year 944 was listed at £22,864, but the 944 Turbo, despite the introduction of three-channel ABS as standard (optional on other models), was far from cheap at £34,168. By comparison, the five-speed 924S was £18,464, while Porsche prices in general now ranged up to £90,000 - the cost of a decent house!

1986 had been another record sales year in the States, despite the higher prices introduced as a result of exchange rate fluctuation. 30,471 Porsches were sold in all (about 58% of production), the 944 and 944S accounting for 10,296 units, while the 944 Turbo found 6215 new buyers.

The 924S was eventually introduced to the American market in June 1986 as an early 1987 model priced at $19,900, some $5600 cheaper than a basic 944 and more than $13,000 less than a Turbo. In US trim, the 924S engine developed 147bhp and 140lbft of torque - the same figures as those for the 944.

Writing for *Car & Driver*, Csaba Csere summed up the 924S as follows: "Some of the faithful may hesitate at first, concerned that the S is a dead ringer for one of the pretenders of the past. But the true believers, who cherish performance above all else, will conclude that its superb balance, beautiful driving qualities, and high-speed capabilities make the new 924S

*A 1987 model year 944 Turbo with 16-inch Fuchs alloy wheels. Note the windscreen wipers, modified after complaints that they lifted off the glass at speeds in excess of 125mph (200kph) - seriously! Washer nozzles were heated from 1985.*

worthy of wearing the Porsche crest."

The 944 Turbo gained ABS braking (optional on the other 944s) and dual airbags, thus becoming the first car in America to offer an airbag on the passenger side. This naturally meant a new four-spoke steering wheel was required, while a panel had to be made in the top of the fascia for the passenger side as a consequence.

Extended road test reports are extremely useful; most magazines get to try a vehicle for around 1000 miles in a short space of time, whereas extended use provides a much clearer picture of a car's character. *Road & Track* noted that the 944 Turbo objected to town work (especially from cold), but loved long country runs. This was quite an important consideration for anyone considering a 944 purely to commute across town on a daily basis. Nevertheless, following a comparison test which brought together the 924S, 944, 944S and 944 Turbo at the Willow Springs race track, the same journal gave the turbocharged car a convincing thumbs-up if price was not considered as part of the equation. Interestingly, the magazine felt that the 924S offered

*Another 1987 Turbo, this time in standard trim and very tasteful surroundings.*

*German advertising for the 1987 Porsche Turbo Cup series. As can be seen from the fixture list, it was extended to ten rounds and no longer limited to domestic tracks.*

*A 250bhp Turbo Cup racer prepared for the 1987 season.*

*Turbo Cup action from the Salzburgring in August 1987.*

by far the best value, followed by the Turbo, 944 and 944S, in that order.

Early 1987 saw a lot of speculation in the press regarding the forthcoming 984, and a number of interesting four-cylinder prototype shots. The new model was supposed to take up a market position somewhere in between the existing 924/944 range and the 911, perhaps being powered by a water-cooled flat-four in the rear, and maybe sourced from VW. Plans for the Boxster had still not been approved at this stage, but there was a lot of activity in Stuttgart nonetheless.

## Boardroom drama

In America, sales of all German cars suffered in 1987. Figures for the 944 and 944S were down by about 20%, while the 944 Turbo suffered a drop of almost 60% compared to the previous year. The main reason for this poor showing was the strong deutschmark, which had moved 23% against the dollar in just 12 months, pushing prices up even further.

At the end of 1987, in the wake of dwindling profits (although the currencies had moved 23%, prices in the States would only bear a 14% increase), a press release stated: "The Supervisory Board of Dr Ing. h.c. F. Porsche AG has announced that Mr Peter W. Schutz and Porsche AG have mutually agreed that Mr Schutz will resign from his position as Chairman of the Executive Board effective 31 December 1987.

"Mr Heinz Branitzki, Deputy Chairman of the Executive Board since 1976, was elected by the Supervisory Board yesterday [16 December] to be the new Chairman of the Executive

*Following the departure of Peter Schutz, Heinz Branitzki became Porsche's new Chairman. After a spell at Carl Zeiss, Branitzki had been with the Stuttgart company since 1965 and had controlled its finances since 1972.*

*The American spec 944 for the 1988 model year.*

*A 1988 944 Turbo for the US market. In sharp contrast to the turbocharged road rocket, Porsche sales in the States were now painfully slow.*

Board as of 1 January 1988."

Schutz was determined to save the 911, which he did very successfully, but he also allowed the company to become almost reliant on the American market. Although the US had always been of immense importance, Ferry Porsche had quite deliberately kept this share of production under 50%, as he didn't want to rely too heavily on sales in one country. Over 60% of production was destined for America by the end of Schutz's tenure, and with an unfavourable exchange rate, this was a disastrous situation which happened to coincide with the Stock Market Crash, an additional problem for the luxury car maker. As regards world economy, no-one could blame him for that; it's worth noting that the events of October 1987, at least in percentage terms, were twice as bad as those of the Wall Street Crash of the late 1920s. And we all know what that led to ... The future looked grim, but Ferry Porsche was positive there was still a market for the Stuttgart thoroughbreds.

Interestingly, rumours of Schutz's departure had been circulating around the industry for some time, and Ferdinand Piech was being put forward in some quarters as a possible replacement. Ironically, despite his close links with Porsche, both through previous experience and family bloodlines, Piech was officially made Chairman of Audi on the same day as Branitzki took up his new position.

## The 1988 model year

For the 1988 model year, the price of all Porsche's four-cylinder models shot up in Germany, thus having a damning effect on sales, at home and in export markets in particular. In price-sensitive America, after a few options had been added, a 944 was about the same price as a hard-charging Maserati Biturbo, whilst competition from Japan was very strong. The Nissan 300ZX Turbo, Mitsubishi Starion Turbo, Mazda RX-7 (either in Turbo or leather-trimmed convertible guise) and Toyota's Supra Turbo were all significantly cheaper, offering reliable high-performance and a well-equipped cockpit as standard.

As *Car & Driver*'s Rich Ceppos said: "Personally, I think Porsche has a problem. While we've been busily putting the Weissach *Wunderkinds* on pedestals, their prices have been creeping steadily skyward. These days,

> **Standard coachwork colours (1988 MY)**
> Black, Guards Red, Azure Blue, Alpine White.
>
> **Special coachwork colours**
> Nougat Brown Metallic, Maraschino Red Metallic, Almond Metallic, Satin Black Metallic, Nile Green Metallic, Ocean Blue Metallic, Stone Grey Metallic, Zermatt Silver Metallic.
>
> **Trim materials**
> Black, burgundy or light grey leatherette with matching inlays. Alternatively, inlays could be in pinstripe velour (black with white, burgundy with white or light grey with white); seat facings could also be supplied in pinstripe flannel cloth (in the same shades as the velour inlays), black, burgundy or light grey 'Porsche' cloth or leather as an option. Carpets came in black, brown, burgundy or light grey.

*A German registered 944 from 1988. The shape remained fairly modern, despite origins dating back to the mid-1970s.*

*Rear view of the same car. In a bid to standardize power units for all markets, a lower compression ratio meant the European 944 now produced 160bhp instead of 163. The revised engine was duly fitted to the 924S, giving that model a welcome power boost.*

just looking at a Porsche price sticker gives me altitude sickness."

After a 23% decline in US sales in 1987, sales fell another 32% the following year to just 16,000 units. As part of a major management shake-up in the US operation, Brian Bowler was given the post of PCNA's new President, but in reality John Cook (the ex-BMW of North America boss who had headed the Reno office since its inception) could hardly be blamed for the poor exchange rates and general downturn in world economy.

As always, the engineers in Stuttgart had prescribed a number of yearly revisions. Central locking became standard in all countries, as did an oil level indicator; the front brake discs and ABS system were improved, while the American spec 944S gained dual airbags. However, the biggest changes were reserved for the standard 944.

With new pistons and a lower 10.2:1 compression ratio, the engine was designed to produce 160bhp in all markets. Maximum power (158bhp in America) was produced at 5900rpm, while 155lbft of torque was developed at 4500rpm, or 3000rpm in the USA. Although this looks like a massive difference in the revs at which peak torque occurred, the reality is that the torque curve was so flat, it didn't really make all that much difference on the road.

These new figures represented a small drop in power for Europe, where the engine carried the M44/09 designation, but a decent gain for the Americans (who received the

*The 1988 model year 944S.*

*Another shot of the 944S. For 1988, 16v models supplied to the UK market inherited the Turbo's underbody rear spoiler.*

*A German registered 944 Turbo. Turbocharged models destined for British shores received disc-type alloys (which could be finished in a platinum colour instead of the usual silver for 1988) as standard equipment.*

M44/10); both markets continued to use their own version of the familiar 016 manual transmission (the three-speed automatic was still listed as an option). The 924S was also given this revised unit, incidentally, along with the 016J or K gearbox.

In Britain, the standard 944 was now listed at £24,237; the 16v model was priced at £26,994, while the Turbo commanded another £9086 on top of that. The addition of a cassette/coin holder as standard on all UK cars and the option of a Panasonic CD player (with or without the ten-speaker audio system) on the Turbo hardly made up the gap in specifications when the 944 was compared to its rivals.

With the 3.6 litre Jaguar XJ-S becoming more sporting in character, and with prices starting at £23,821, it offered not only excellent value-for-money, but masses of power and torque and a more than reasonable turn of speed, too. It was yet another tough player to add to the growing list of cheaper alternatives that offered similar or better performance.

Following Black Monday and the subsequent demise of the Yuppie, one had to wonder how much longer Porsche could trade on its name. Enthusiasts of the marque would always provide the Stuttgart manufacturer with a strong customer base, but the average Yuppie (with inflated income acquired through share dealing at the height of the boom) just wanted a status symbol with which to impress friends. When the market crashed, the demise of the Yuppie was as swift as a 911 Turbo. The end of the breed was no great loss to the general public, but the effects - a sharp downturn in sales - were sorely felt at Porsche and BMW dealerships.

By the way, a limited edition 944 had been launched in September 1987 to mark production of 100,000 944s. Finished in Zermatt Silver Metallic or Satin Black Metallic (with black trim

*Having tried the Turbo in 1988, the respected journalist, Roger Bell, was moved enough to say: "As a 911 fan (and owner), the 944 Turbo left me wondering if I'd got it right ... No car is worth £36,000, but the blown 944 gets close."*

*Two new 944s were announced in December 1987: the Cabriolet (left) and the Turbo S (also known as the Turbo SE). The convertible was expected to go into production for the 1989 season, so was built to generate advance orders, but the equally stunning Turbo S was made available almost straight away.*

combined with Studio cloth inlays and grey carpets), 930 were built, of which only 30 examples of this high specification model made it to the UK.

## Special Turbo models

Early 1988 saw the launch of what, for many, was the ultimate development of the 944 series - the Turbo SE (known as the Turbo S in America). Based on the Turbo Cup model, the £41,000 machine came with a 250bhp engine, uprated brakes and suspension, a limited-slip differential, and a number of unique features including special forged alloy wheels.

The power unit, designated M44/52, developed 250bhp at 6000rpm and 258lbft of torque at 4000rpm, the increase being achieved by adopting a modified KKK (Kuhnle, Kopp & Kausch) blower, turning up the boost to 11.9psi and recalibrating the engine management system. This was linked to a 016R five-speed gearbox and 3.38:1 final-drive ratio: according to Porsche, the SE was capable of covering 0-60 in 5.7 seconds before going on to a top speed of 161mph - as far as production cars go, only the Porsche 928 S4, Lamborghini Countach, and Ferrari's GTO and Testarossa were quicker.

In line with increased horsepower, the model was given adjustable Koni gas-filled shock absorbers, stiffer springs and torsion bars, a thicker 26.5mm (1.04in) diameter front anti-roll bar, and harder suspension bushes; an lsd and bigger brakes completed the highly desirable package. The braking system was actually sourced from the 928, incorporating ABS and massive

*The Turbo S quickly acquired an enviable reputation, thanks to its outright speed combined with superb handling characteristics. 1000 limited edition cars were built, plus another 635 to the same mechanical specification. Although advance order books were due to close in August 1988, the elegant Cabriolet model would ultimately be delayed for a number of reasons.*

discs - 305mm at the front and 300mm at the rear (12 and 11.8in, respectively). The seven-spoke alloys, 7J x 16 up front and 9J x 16 at the back, came with 225/50 and 245/45-section VR-rated tyres.

The limited edition models were painted in an attractive Silber Rosa shade and trimmed in a rather less successful burgundy-coloured Studio cloth. They came with the option of 'Turbo' graphics on the offside front wing, but power-assisted steering, air conditioning, side rubbing strips, a rear wiper, graduated windscreen, ten-speaker stereo, power windows and mirrors, power front seats with split rears, and headlight beam adjustment and washing system came as standard in all markets.

The *Autocar* described it as "Porsche's best-sorted car," while the tester for *MotorSport*, despite reservations about certain areas of the package, was sufficiently moved to say that "at the end of a full day of hustling along B-roads, the driver's smile of contentment tells all."

The 944 Turbo S was launched in America halfway through the 1988 model year at $45,275. Like its European counterpart, it had a fully-loaded specification (although, rather cheekily, the sunroof, cruise control and Blaupunkt stereo radio/cassette were listed as mandatory extras at $2157) and, courtesy of 247bhp at 6000rpm and 258lbft of torque at 4000rpm, absolutely stunning performance - 0-60 in 5.5 seconds, and a top speed of 162mph (259kph).

Despite the high price, *Car &*

*The end of the 924S (this 1988 model has the optional alloy wheels, by the way) meant the 944 would have to provide entry-level Porsche motoring from now on. More than 150,000 924s had been built by the time production came to an end.*

## How fast it gets from o always been an importa

If you were so inclined, you could go out right now and buy yourself a new Porsche 944 or 944 Turbo, roll it out of the showroom, gas it up, enter it in a certified Showroom Stock event and do with it exactly what nature intended.

Race it.

Of course, you'd have to go to racing school and get your license first.

*Helmuth Bott - Porsche's technical supremo, pictured in 1985, the year in which he stated that the 959's four-wheel drive system would be adopted on the 944 and 928 in time, but it never was, of course. After his retirement in September 1988, Professor Bott was replaced by Dr Ulrich Bez as Technical Director (Bez had been a Porsche employee in the past, but had spent much of his recent career with BMW). At the same time, it was announced that Horst Marchart had been made responsible for road car development (Tony Lapine remained head of styling), Wolfhelm Gorissen, Bott's former assistant, now dealt with outside consultancy work, and Rainer Frock was put in charge of the Weissach facility.*

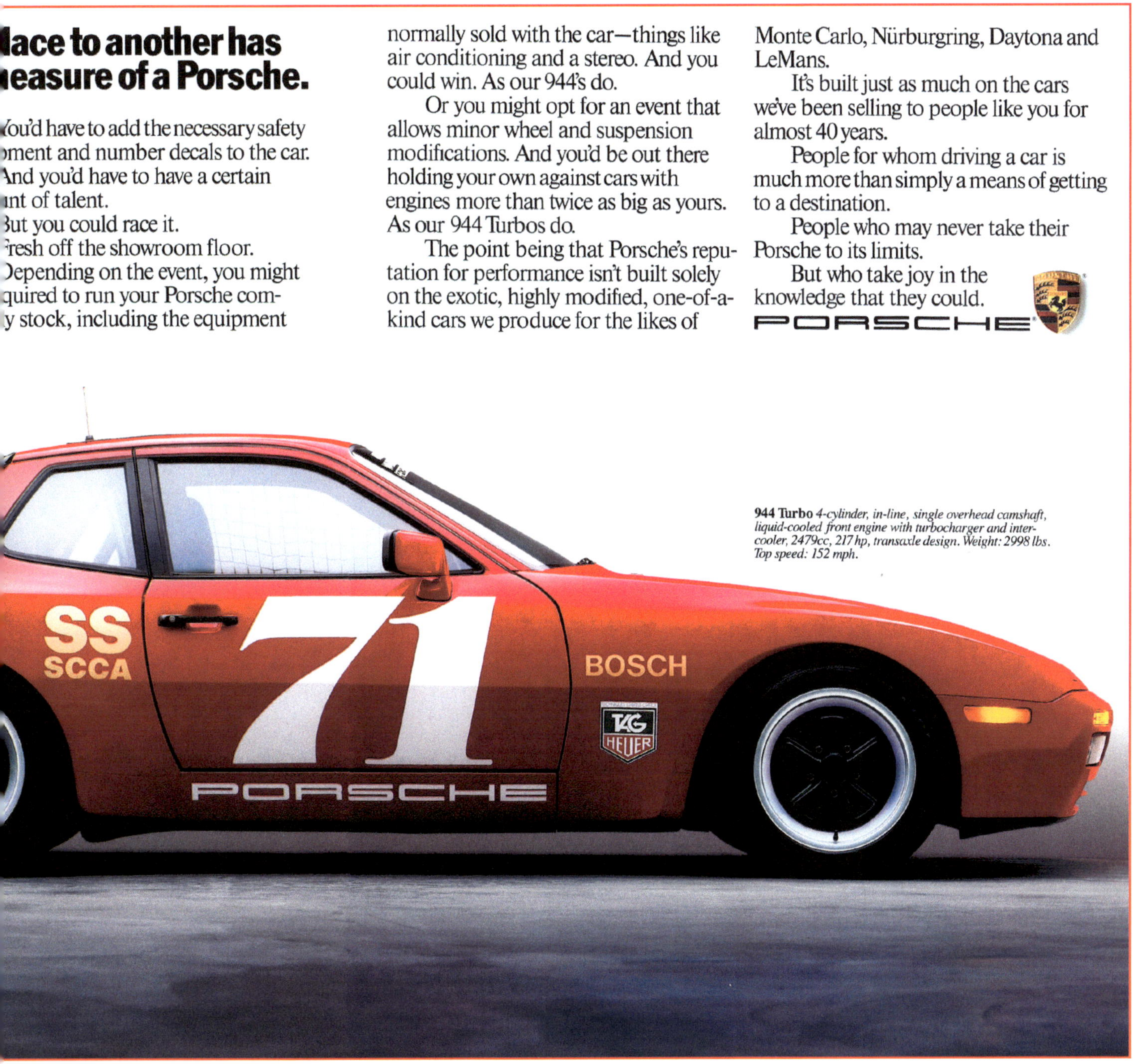

*American advertising showing an SCCA racer based on the 944 Turbo. The SCCA and IMSA-run events brought a great deal of publicity for manufacturers, especially if their exploits on the track were successful.*

...ace to another has ...easure of a Porsche.

...ou'd have to add the necessary safety ...ment and number decals to the car. ...nd you'd have to have a certain ...nt of talent.
...ut you could race it.
...resh off the showroom floor.
...epending on the event, you might ...quired to run your Porsche com-...y stock, including the equipment normally sold with the car—things like air conditioning and a stereo. And you could win. As our 944's do.

Or you might opt for an event that allows minor wheel and suspension modifications. And you'd be out there holding your own against cars with engines more than twice as big as yours. As our 944 Turbos do.

The point being that Porsche's reputation for performance isn't built solely on the exotic, highly modified, one-of-a-kind cars we produce for the likes of Monte Carlo, Nürburgring, Daytona and LeMans.

It's built just as much on the cars we've been selling to people like you for almost 40 years.

People for whom driving a car is much more than simply a means of getting to a destination.

People who may never take their Porsche to its limits.

But who take joy in the knowledge that they could.

PORSCHE

**944 Turbo** 4-cylinder, in-line, single overhead camshaft, liquid-cooled front engine with turbocharger and intercooler, 2479cc, 217 hp, transaxle design. Weight: 2998 lbs. Top speed: 152 mph.

# Before we start product[ion] on a car, it's already finis[hed.]

The car on the left is the 944 GTP. In 1981, we entered it in the Twenty-Four Hours of Le Mans where it competed against cars with engines more than twice the size of its own in-line four.

Skeptics doubted it would finish, let alone place in the top ten. It was, after all, a David among scores of Goliaths.

Nevertheless, it came in an astonishing seventh overall. And spent less time in the pits than any other car in the race.

It was this car's superb racing performance that led, in 1982, to the introduction of the production 944. A car which our engineers have continued to scrutinize, to amend, to push, to mold into the car on the right.

The 944 Turbo.

A car with a top speed of 152 mph, 217 horsepower, and the ability to accelerate from 0 to 60 in just 6.1 second[s.]

A car which, even six years later, still bears a remarkable resemblance t[o] the Le Mans prototype to which it owe[s] much of its original technology.

For us, competition provides a co[n]stant source of challenge and new idea[s.] And we'll continue to race Porsches fo[r] as long as we continue to build Porsch[es.]

Not because we have any particu[lar]

**944 GTP** *4-cylinder, in-line, two overhead camshafts, four valves per cylinder, liquid-cooled front engine with turbocharger, 2479cc, 410 hp. Weight: 2094 lbs. Top speed: 185+ mph.*

*Another piece of competition-based advertising from the States, this time showing the 1981 Le Mans car alongside the 944 Turbo. This dated from early 1988, almost seven years after the racer first appeared at the famous Sarthe track.*

*Driver* noted: "It's by far the strongest-performing four-cylinder car in the world, and only a few cars of any stripe can match or beat its numbers. The same holds true for its combination of mechanical smoothness, creature comforts, and handling precision. Add all its virtues together and its least expensive competitor is the Porsche 928 S4, which, comparably equipped, costs another twenty grand. See? We told you the 944 Turbo S is a bargain."

Over at *Road & Track*, the high price, sluggish off-boost response, and engine and road noise were listed as dislikes, but the on-boost power, high level of grip, excellent brakes and good handling balance seemed to more than make up for them.

Although at the time of the initial announcement, mention was only eed to chalk up more wins than we've already accumulated.

But because when we introduce a performance car, we like to be sure it's going to perform.

If you'd like to receive a free full-color booklet detailing the Porsche 924S and 944 series, simply give us a call at (800) 252-4444, extension 304.

PORSCHE

**944 Turbo** *4-cylinder, in-line, single overhead camshaft, liquid-cooled front engine with turbocharger and intercooler, 2479cc, 217 hp, transaxle design. Weight: 2998 lbs. Top speed: 152 mph.*

made of the limited run of 1000 cars painted in Silber Rosa, a total of 1635 were built to the same mechanical specification in the end, with 718 of them going to the States; only 70 made it to British shores. For the record, the extra 635 were finished in standard colours and trim.

## Demise of the 924

Some were predicting that the 924/944 series could continue for another six or seven years, but with mediocre reviews and a flood of fresh competition, combined with the news that production had been dramatically cut back (by as much as 30%, in fact, although rumours regarding Porsche abandoning the Neckarsulm works were fervently denied), it became increasingly obvious that, at the very least, the 924S's days were numbered. There were still several developments outlined for the 944, but it was disturbingly quiet on the 924 front. Indeed, after a close shave in 1985, the 924 series was finally discontinued in July 1988. However, more than 150,000 units had been built, so although it didn't attain the success that was projected 13 years earlier, it was far from a failure.

Was another 'cheap' model the way forward? A Porsche official noted: "It's a vicious circle. We want to build an affordable sports car. That means big volume and lots of proprietary parts. But as soon as you do that, the quality and prestige of the product suffers. We learned our lesson with the old Volks-Porsche 914, and with the original 924. Today, the management won't accept any car unless it's 100% Porsche."

Although prototypes were built, ultimately, the amount of investment needed to get such a project off the ground - not just in terms of R&D, but a new factory to handle the level of production necessary to make it viable - simply didn't make commercial sense. A deciding factor was the strong deutschmark; having been around 3.5 DM to $1 at the start of 1985, three years later it stood at less than 1.7 DM. In this price-sensitive end of the market, too many compromises would have had to be made to keep costs down.

As the deutschmark continued to strengthen, Porsche decided to adopt a policy of going even more upmarket. In order to see any kind of profit on cheaper models, prices in export markets would have to be such that the cars would be uncompetitive. Although for most this meant the end of their dream of Porsche ownership, in reality, it was the only logical answer.

## Racing in America

Although Porsche had used the 924 to launch a successful all-out assault on the Sports Car Club of America (SCCA) series, the 944 didn't really need the publicity. Indeed, the model probably had more to lose than gain if results were not as good as its reputation promised. This probably goes some way towards explaining the introduction of the Turbo Cup series. Nonetheless, Al Holbert, who headed the motorsport section at PCNA, decided to campaign a 525bhp spaceframe car, entered as a 944 GTR.

141

*Meanwhile, in Europe, the Turbo Cup soldiered on into 1989 (indeed, the 944s provided a support race at Le Mans that year), only to be replaced by the Carrera Cup - campaigned by 911s - in 1990. However, 944s have continued to feature in club events.*

It failed to impress at the 1985 SCCA Run-Offs, and, despite a substantial increase in power for the following year, results were not forthcoming. Changes in the regulations further complicated matters, prompting the premature end of the GTR.

Meanwhile, standard cars were having a little more success. The normally-aspirated Carlsen Racing 944 won the 1986 SCCA Escort Endurance Series Championship (S/S GT) title, while at the 1987 SCCA Run-Offs, Freddy Baker took Showroom Stock GT honours with a 944 Turbo, repeating the feat the following year.

David Finch claimed the 1988 GT2 title driving a 944S, and held on to lift the trophy again in 1989. However, the S/S GT category fell to a Chevrolet Camaro at Road Atlanta that October, thus bringing the Stuttgart marque's winning run to an end.

There was still a great deal of activity surrounding the 944 series at the Porsche workshops in Germany - new engines, and the prospect of the long-awaited convertible (in fact, advance orders were being taken for the latter from the beginning of 1988). For the time being at least, it looked as if the model's future was secure.

# 6

## THE TWILIGHT YEARS

As noted in the previous chapter, the 924S was discontinued and did not appear in the 1989 line-up. More changes were planned.

Branitzski, the brains behind the company's finances for many years, wanted to take the remaining four-cylinder range further upmarket in order to enhance Porsche prestige, and make the business more profitable in the face of falling sales. "No-one has ever dared doubt the engineering integrity of the marque," said *Performance Car*, "but doubts did begin to surface when fairly ordinary four-cylinder Porsches began to creep up to extraordinary prices: the bubble eventually burst last year when the magic of the Porsche name had worn thin when matched against mediocre specifications at prohibitive prices.

"The new 2.7 litre 944 is Porsche's bid to restore performance to the core of Porsche appeal. New Chairman Heinz Branitzki has axed the 'entry-level' 924 - the car that traded most heavily on the Porsche name - and uprated the whole of the 944 range.

"Our test car, the 'base' 944, thus takes over the entry-level mantle but rises from 2.5 litres and 160bhp to 2.7 and 165; the 16-valve 944S takes a bigger jump - from 2.5 to a full 3.0 litres and 211bhp - while the top Turbo, still at 2.5 litres, is now a 160mph machine. Prices rise to a whisker under £26,000 for the plain model."

### The 1989 model year in detail

When the 1989 model year range was announced in August 1988, many expected the 944 to receive a three-litre powerplant, easily the world's largest displacement for a four-cylinder engine at that time. Cubic capacity did increase, sure enough, though only to 2681cc, achieved by leaving the stroke at 78.9mm but taking the bore out another 4mm to 104mm.

With a 10.9:1 compression ratio, a different camshaft, a new inlet manifold and slightly larger diameter inlet valves, the 2.7 litre engine (designated M44/13) developed 165bhp at 5800rpm and a healthy 166lbft of torque at 4200rpm. Not surprisingly, the proven Bosch L-Jetronic fuel-injection and Motronic (DME) ignition system employed on the 2.5 litre models were kept, although modified for their new application.

Linked to the same 016J five-speed gearbox and 3.89:1 final-drive, the European version was expected to cover 0-60 in 8.2 seconds and go on to a top speed of 137mph (219kph), according to factory figures. The automatic transmission option continued, although the three-speeder was starting to show its age by now and the 0-60 time slipped to 9.4 seconds - rather pedestrian performance for the standards of the day, it has to be said.

The suspension was carried over from the previous model, along with the braking system (although ABS braking was now standard across the range, with asbestos-free pads employed in all markets) and wheel and tyre combination.

With no changes prescribed for the body, it was hard to tell the difference between a 1988 and 1989 car

*For 1989, the 944 received a 2.7 litre engine, although there was little to distinguish the latest model from the outside.*

Another view of the 2.7 litre car. The 'Telephone Dial' wheels were carried over, and it can be seen in this picture that even the badging remained the same as that of its predecessor.

The 1989 MY 944 Turbo, seen here sporting the optional wing graphics (like the 924 Carrera GT, when specified, the decal was applied on one side only). The 250bhp engine and the uprated chassis components that went with it (including the forged seven-spoke alloys) were now standard for the turbocharged model.

*Interior of the home market 944 Turbo for 1989.*

*Although not a good way to discourage drinking and driving, this 1989 picture does at least show how practical the 944 series was for a sports coupé.*

*A pre-production version of the S2 coupé, the smoother Turbo-style nose being a feature. Only 12,831 of the old 2.5 litre 944S models were produced, with 8703 of them finding buyers in America.*

*Tail of the pre-production car. At this stage, the badging had yet to be updated, and the use of the cast 'Telephone Dial' alloy wheels would be limited to the base 944 model once the specification sheets had been finalized.*

# 944 S 2 Cabriolet

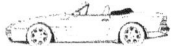

**Motor – Querschnitt**
engine – cross section
moteur – coupe transversale
motore – sezione trasversale

*This cutaway drawing of the S2 power unit shows the narrow valve angle, with the valves operated by twin-overhead camshafts. Rated at 211bhp, with its improved breathing the 16v engine would happily rev to the 6500rpm red-line.*

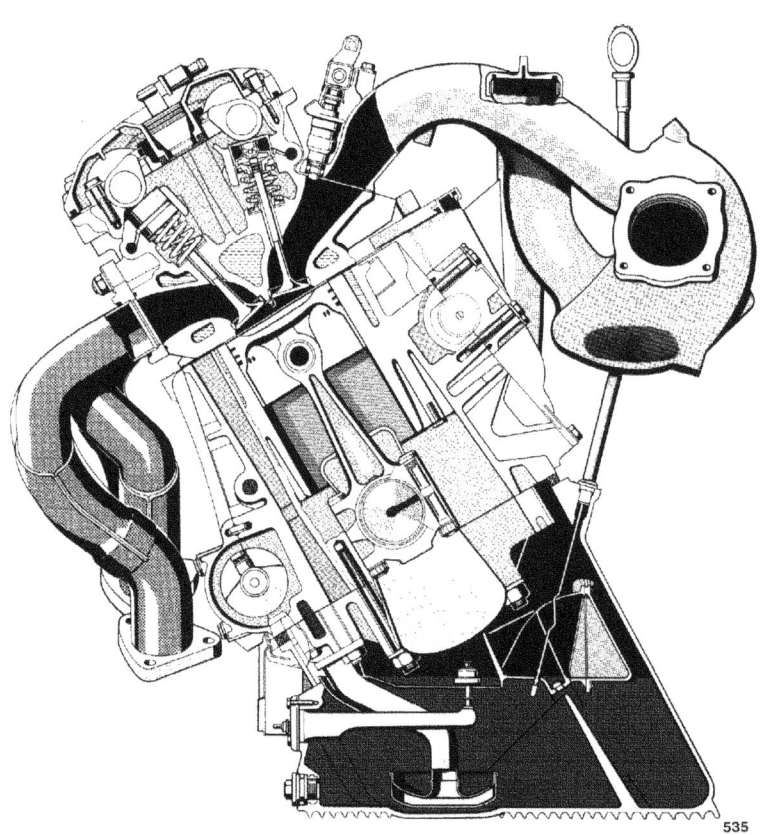

*Viewed from the side, this cutaway reveals the two inlet and two exhaust valves employed for each of the four cylinders. It also shows the much smaller than usual water jackets, and the distributor driven off the front of the engine in a bid to reduce height (the latter has been a feature on all 944 powerplants).*

# 944 S2 Cabriolet

Motor – Längsschnitt
engine – longitudinal section
moteur – coupe longitudinale
motore – sezione longitudinale

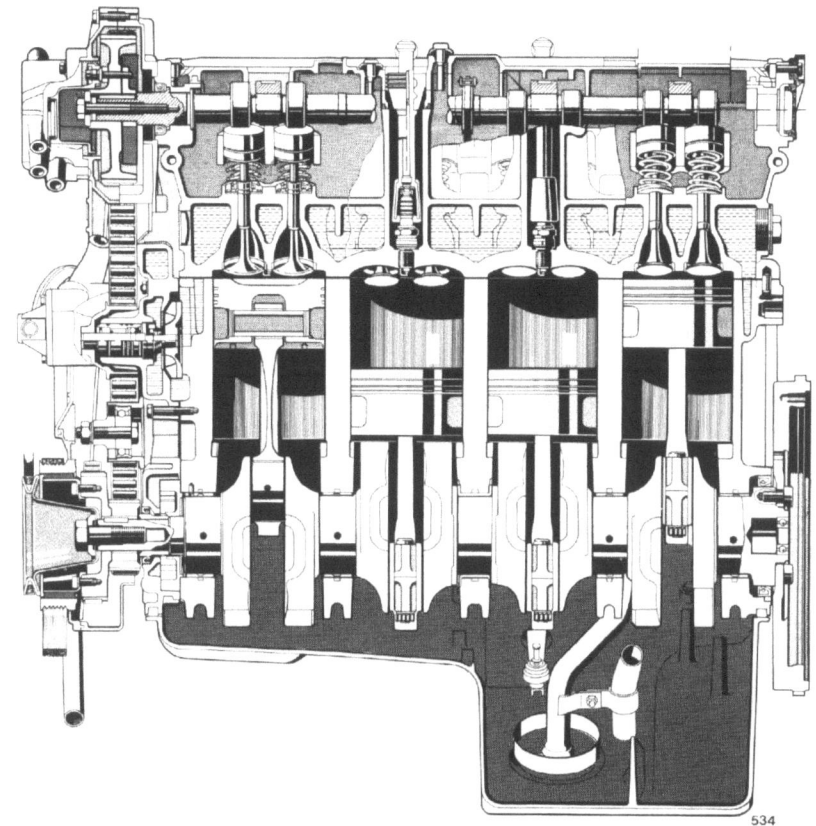

*The S2 models inherited the suspension and braking system from the old 220bhp Turbo, so handling and roadholding were pretty exceptional by any standard.*

without driving it. It was then that the engineer's work became evident: "The 2.7 is noticeably more characterful at high revs than any previous unblown 944," said *Autocar & Motor*. "Beyond 4000rpm, its exhaust takes on an attractive Alfasud-like rasp that makes exploiting its considerable, solidly delivered performance an enjoyable pastime."

*The 1989 S2 coupé as it appeared in the showrooms, complete with the forged disc-type alloy wheels. To match the brutal looks of the machine, the exhaust note was much heavier than on the previous 16v car.*

As part of the plan to enhance the appeal of the 944 line, the 250bhp Turbo S/SE described in the last chapter became the standard turbocharged model for 1989 (after all, the power output from the new three-litre unit was perhaps too close to the 220bhp of the earlier Turbo), equipped with a three-way catalytic converter for all markets.

*Fast Lane* reported: "In the cockpit, there is precious little to remind you that you are driving the new model. The difference is only noted if you are in a great hurry or on a bad road. In the first case, apart from enjoying the extra power, you will appreciate the uprated suspension which, if you push the car to its limits, provides even more precise handling with very little roll.

"On bad roads, however, the suspension leaves no doubts about the surface the wheels have to deal with, especially if you drive slowly. Nevertheless, thanks to the well-contoured seats, the shaking the occupants are submitted to remains quite acceptable."

However, the biggest change for 1989 concerned the 944S's replacement - the three-litre 944 S2. The S2 was given the Turbo body modifications and disc-type alloy wheels (7J items with 205/55 ZR16 tyres at the front, and 225/50s

> **Standard coachwork colours (1989 MY)**
> Black, Guards Red, Azure Blue, Alpine White.
>
> **Special coachwork colours**
> Light Gold Metallic, Velvet Red Metallic, Glacier Blue Metallic, Satin Black Metallic, Linen Grey Metallic, Baltic Blue Metallic, Stone Grey Metallic, Zermatt Silver Metallic.
>
> **Trim materials**
> Black, blue, burgundy or linen grey leatherette with matching inlays. Alternatively, inlays could be in pinstripe velour (black with white, blue with white, burgundy with white or linen grey with white); seat facings could also be supplied in black, blue, burgundy or linen grey 'Porsche' cloth, Studio Check cloth or leather as an option. Carpets came in black, brown, burgundy or light grey.

mounted on 8J rims at the rear) but, as is so often the case with Porsche, it was the engine that received the majority of attention. The M44/41 unit was the result of almost two years' development and over 50,000 miles (80,000km) of road testing. The cylinder liners were siamesed, while the water jackets were raised to effectively cool only the top part of the bores, enabling the engineers to dramatically reduce the amount of coolant needed (lessons learnt from the TAG F1 project compensated for this by spraying oil onto the undersides of the pistons). A new forged crankshaft ran in the highly-modified, lighter and stiffer alloy block, and gave the engine a longer 88mm stroke; combined with the same bore measurement as that employed for the new 2.7 litre unit, this gave a displacement of 2990cc.

With four valves per cylinder, revised camshafts, the latest L-Jetronic EFI and Motronic engine management system, and a compression ratio of 10.9:1 (achieved by new forged pistons, both lighter and shorter than before, connected to the crankshaft by forged conrods instead of the former cast items), the additional 511cc endowed the S2 with 211bhp at 5800rpm and a peak torque figure of 207lbft at 4100rpm - the latter representing a 22% increase over the original 16v unit.

When production started, the aluminium alloy sump was replaced by a lightweight SMC one with a larger capacity; thus, the S2 became the first production car in the world to feature this component in plastic. Like the Turbo, it employed an oil cooler instead of the oil/water heat exchanger used on the other 944s.

The 083F five-speed transmission was unique to the S2, with the same ratios as the Turbo 'box on the four lower gears, but a new 0.78:1 fifth combined with an equally new 3.87:1 final-drive. Only 66lbs (30kg) heavier than a standard 944, and the same amount lighter than a Turbo, Porsche figures quoted a top speed of 149mph (238kph) and a 0-60 time of 6.9 seconds.

With the increased performance, the S2 was fitted with the outgoing Turbo model's brakes (the 1989 Turbo had the larger S/SE front discs, of course) and suspension, although for those who wanted the ultimate in handling, it was possible to uprate the chassis to the latest Turbo specifications. On the other hand, the S2 was quite capable of returning up to 41mpg on a steady throttle.

In line with Branitzski's policies, 1989 MY prices rose by quite some margin. The standard 944 was now DM 65,865, while the Turbo commanded the best part of DM 40,000 more - the latter represented a DM 16,000 increase in a year! The newly-introduced S2, meanwhile, started at DM 74,965. An automatic gearbox could only be specified on the basic 944.

Meanwhile, the 911 had received a major facelift with the arrival of the 1989 Carrera 4. The whole 911 range duly adopted this new body style over the next year or so, receiving the Type 964 designation in the process.

## The American market

The 1989 model year range was launched in the States in September 1988. The US spec 2.7 litre 944 was endowed with 162bhp at 5800rpm, and the same maximum torque as that quoted for its European counterpart. It also had the same 016J five-speed transmission and 3.89:1 final-drive, so performance was very similar - independent tests timed the 0-60 dash at 7.5 seconds, with the quarter-mile marker coming up 8.2 seconds later (obviously, Porsche's reputation for giving out conservative figures was still justified).

Priced at $36,360, it came with ABS, automatic temperature control, a power sunroof, central locking, electrically-operated seat height adjustment, cruise control, a Blaupunkt stereo radio/cassette, power windows and mirrors, and an alarm. With all these items as standard, not surprisingly, a larger capacity alternator was fitted for 1989.

*Road & Track* observed: "The extra 15bhp transforms the 944's character to that of a more muscular and extroverted car ... Those who hope to equal or surpass the Porsche's qualities have their work cut out for them. The 944 simply has a rock-solid depth of engineering and an honesty of purpose that resist imitation."

The $47,600 Turbo gave the 247bhp and 258lbft found on last year's Turbo S, along with limited-slip differential, harder suspension and forged seven-spoke alloys. Like the European models, although the gearbox was different to the version used on the 220bhp cars, the internal ratios were the same, and the 3.38:1 final-drive was retained.

In the US, the three-litre S2 unit

*The four-cylinder line-up pictured in 1989, with S2s to the fore. Behind them, the 944 Turbo can be seen on the left, with the basic 2.7 litre model on the right.*

*A 2.7 litre 944 for the American 1989 model year, seen here fitted with the optional forged alloys. ('Telephone Dial' wheels were standard for the basic 944, as in Europe, although the US spec vehicles continued to be fitted with wider 215/60-section rubber.)*

*The hard-charging 944 Turbo S, launched in America halfway through the 1988 model year, became the standard 944 Turbo for 1989. This was to be the last full year in which the Turbo was marketed in the States; eventually, a total of 13,892 turbocharged versions of the 944 made it across the Atlantic.*

*The three-litre S2 engine. It can readily be distinguished from its 2.5 litre 16v counterpart by the different 'quadrilateral' intake manifold shape (seen on the far side of this picture).*

gave 208bhp at 5800rpm and 207lbft of torque at 4100rpm, while the rest of the specification was pretty much the same as that found on European models. The S2 coupé, which was capable of 149mph (238kph) and could demolish the 0-60 yardstick in 6.4 seconds, came with automatic temperature control, central locking, electric mirrors and windows, a sunroof, stereo radio/cassette, an alarm, and power passenger seat height adjustment as part of the standard $41,900 package. Oddly, a rear wiper was listed as an extra, priced at $313.

Having tried the S2 for size, *Road & Track* concluded: "Combining the 944's can-do-no-wrong handling with the torque and response of a naturally-aspirated three-litre engine produces in the S2 perhaps the quickest Porsche for driving sinuous roads."

### The S2 in Britain

When interviewed at the 1988 Motor Show, Peter Bulbeck, the MD of Porsche Cars GB, stated that the S2 models were due to arrive in the UK during the spring of 1989. Meanwhile, the 944S quietly disappeared from the price

*A 1989 model year 944 Turbo for the UK market. The Turbo was seriously expensive in Britain - the same money would have bought a V12 Jaguar XJ-S Convertible, a Mercedes-Benz 500SL, De Tomaso Pantera GTS, or even a Maserati Spyder with enough change for a Toyota MR2.*

lists as it had simply failed to take off in Britain.

Following its appraisal of the new range, *MotorSport* noted: "The original 2.5 litre 944S never realised Porsche's expectations because it offered no appreciable gains in performance below 4000rpm, within the realms of speed limits worldwide in other words. The addition of 500cc has changed a great deal now, because although the performance steps up at 4000rpm there is a substantial amount of torque to be had from 2000rpm upwards. As well as that the throttle response is snappier."

Indeed, looking at the torque curve, it peaked at around 2500rpm,

before dropping off slightly until around 3200rpm, when it picked up again. Interestingly, the same journal added: "Three-litres is probably as far as Porsche can go with the four-cylinder engine, despite the twin-balancer shafts, for you can almost feel the individual piston strokes as they merge into a 6000rpm symphony."

In an interview with Jochen Freund (Project Director on both the 924 and 944), it was revealed that the block would, in fact, take up to 3.2 litres, but he felt that three-litres was enough for the four. Sixes had been tried, along with supercharging, but both were dismissed. As a result, Freund expected the engine to remain pretty much the same for at least three years.

In reality, with its greater torque at low revs, the S2 was a much more practical proposition for the congested and increasingly speed-limited roads of the UK (after a great deal of talk, traffic cameras were finally installed and operational in 1992). Prices for the three-litre cars were announced in February: £31,304 for the coupé and a provisional £36,713 for the soft-top.

There were, naturally, a number of options. The most popular items included a limited-slip differential (£741), metallic paint (£664), air conditioning (£1683), an electric sunroof (£1030), full cloth trim with matching door panels (£328), full leather trim (£3425), split rear seats (£358) and cruise control (£394).

Most press members seemed to appreciate the models. However, after a road test of the three-litre coupé, although they felt the S2 was "extremely rewarding to drive hard," *Autocar & Motor* made a valid point that would come back to haunt the Stuttgart firm with the 968: "Curiously, the engine seems almost *too* efficient. It does everything asked of it with remarkable dexterity, propels the car very rapidly and has a subtle twin-cam twang, yet there is something lacking. Apart from outright speed it is unthrilling."

At the same time, the 944 (with central locking, an alarm, full-function power seats and automatic heating control as standard) was £25,990, and just under £40,000 was being asked for the Turbo - slightly less than the 1988 SE, but substantially more than the outgoing 220bhp version.

*Performance Car* compared the 2.7 litre 944 with XJ-S 3.6 and Toyota Supra Turbo just after the new Porsche line-up was introduced. There was no clear-cut winner, but there *was* more bad news for the Stuttgart firm: "The Porsche upholds one of the greatest sports car names of all, yet in an era when even £20,000 buys 150mph, the latest £26,000, 132mph 944 threatens to distort the price/performance balance even more seriously than did the now-deleted 924S. The 944 feels little, if any, better in its 2.7 litre form: worst of all, it appears to have lost out on precious refinement."

A lot of this could have been down to the new engine's torque curve, which was certainly a lot peakier than before.

## A Cabriolet at last

Although it took centre stage on the Porsche stand during the 1988 European show circuit, and advance orders had been taken several months earlier - signifying imminent introduction - production of the long-awaited Cabriolet model did not begin until January 1989.

It was delayed for a number of reasons (waiting for the S2 specifications

160

*Left, top: Although the convertible prototype of 1985 was built by Karosserie Baur (a company perhaps best known for its work on the BMW 2002), the contract for the production models went to ASC, which duly established a factory in Germany.*

*Left, bottom: The S2 Cabriolet. In profile, the shorter windscreen becomes evident, being 60mm (2.4in) lower than that of the coupé. Note the frameless side windows, the lack of rear quarterlights (which dramatically reduced all-round visibility when the hood was raised), deletion of the rear spoiler and the optional forged alloys.*

A vision of beauty. An attractive young lady driving the new Cabriolet.

*Interior of the S2 Cabriolet. The rear seats were retained, despite the hood mechanism, and it was possible to fold down the top part of the seatback to enable longer loads to be carried in the boot. This was a welcome feature as the convertible's trunk was quite small. Leather trim was much cheaper on the drophead model.*

to be introduced, worries over the strong deutschmark and the establishment of ASC's facilities being the main ones), but was duly made available in April that year as an early 1990 model, priced at DM 86,265 (almost DM 10,000 more than the original quote from the opening months of '88).

There were already a number of companies offering soft-top conversions of the 944, but most people who were in the market for an open Porsche waited for the official factory version. After all, the prototype had been shown so long ago, who would have thought it would

*The three-litre power unit installed in the engine bay of the S2.*

*Side view of the S2 Cabriolet as it first appeared in the showroom, complete with the standard 16-inch 'Design 90' seven-spoke alloys specified for the soft-top model. Although the alloys looked like the earlier (and far more expensive) forged items, they were, in fact, cast, and could be identified by the different way in which the spokes merged with the wheel rim. They were fitted to the S2 coupé midway through the 1989 model year as supplies became available.*

*The S2 Cabriolet (with optional disc-type forged alloys) and S2 coupé dating from 1989. With the optional seven-spoke forged alloy wheels, apart from the badging, the S2 looked identical to the 944 Turbo.*

*The Porsche range pictured in 1989.*

*The 1990 model year 944 Turbo. Note the use of 'Design 90' wheels (with 7 and 9J rim widths on the turbocharged car instead of the 7 and 8J combination found on the normally-aspirated range), and the new rear spoiler fitted to the 1990 Turbo (which was adopted on the S2 coupé the following year, incidentally). In contrast to earlier spoilers in this position, it was possible to have this one finished in body colour.*

take years for it to become available?

In reality, the S2 Cabriolet was exactly what Porsche needed to revive its fortunes in the USA. Styled by Tony Lapine, it featured a power-operated hood (although catches had to be manually released first), suitable strengthening of the body (a second floorpan was added, along with additional bracing around the door openings, under the rear seat and across the front of the cockpit), a slightly shorter windscreen and frameless side windows; surprisingly, the design managed to retain the 2+2 seating arrangement found on earlier 944s.

Mechanically, the Cabriolet mirrored the specification of the three-litre coupé, so with only 123lbs (56kg) more weight to carry around - the loss of the rear hatchback almost cancelled out the extra metalwork necessary to keep the body rigid - performance was naturally very similar.

The 1985 prototype was built by Baur, but the conversion and final assembly of the production Cabriolet

*The 1990 Turbo in profile. Sadly, time was running out for the turbocharged coupé.*

*The 1990 MY 944 S2 coupé. Note the modern script used for the model - the first few cars kept the old 944S badge.*

### Standard coachwork colours (1990 MY)
Black, Guards Red, Azure Blue, Alpine White.

### Special coachwork colours
Crystal Silver Metallic, Cyclamen Red Metallic, Baltic Blue Metallic, Titanium Metallic, Glacier Blue Metallic, Velvet Red Metallic, Panther Black Metallic, Linen Grey Metallic.

### Trim materials
Black, blue, burgundy or linen grey leatherette with matching inlays. Alternatively, inlays could be in pinstripe velour (black with white, blue with white, burgundy with white or linen grey with white); seat facings could also be supplied in black, blue, burgundy or linen grey 'Porsche' cloth, Studio Check cloth or leather as an option. Carpets came in black, brown, burgundy or light grey. The Cabriolet hood was available in black, blue or burgundy.

was carried out by the American Sunroof Company (better-known as ASC), at its new factory in Heilbronn, Germany. There were no problems with the quality of ASC's work. As *Motor Trend* pointed out: "Both the recontoured body and the folding top easily meet the standards set by the rest of the car. The top is electric, though not nearly as zoot as the all-power unit on the 911. The actual latching mechanism requires some driver participation; a pair of wrenches key into the latches that secure the top to the windshield." It added: "The 944 provides its own mechanical entertainment, as the side windows automatically slide to the halfway mark as the top rises into position." Regarding the rigidity of the vehicle, the same magazine reported: "The Cabrio is nearly as tight as the coupé, and with the top up, it's nearly as quiet as the original. You'd be hard pressed to discern any cowl shake, just a bit of flex in the steering column. Even hard cornering won't produce any creaks or groans."

Introduced at $48,600, it came with power seats, heated and electrically-adjustable door mirrors, dual airbags, automatic climate control, a four-speaker stereo radio/cassette, and cruise control as standard. Leather trim was only $615 extra.

## The 1990 model year
Following a luke-warm response to the new 2.7 litre model (let's face it, 1989 was a pretty spectacular year for new car introductions!), the standard 944 was discontinued in the middle of 1989. A total of 117,790 944s had been built since 1981, of which, no less than 71,311 went to the States. Add on all the variants, and the 944 was easily Porsche's most successful model in terms of sales.

There was still life in the 944 theme yet, though, with a number of minor changes being outlined for the series. Engine electronics were updated on the S2 unit, and full emissions equipment was fitted for all markets in response to newly-introduced European regulations (although power and torque output figures were unchanged); all models now came with the 'Design 90' wheels.

For the 1990 model year, the S2 coupé was priced at just over DM 78,000 (around DM 12,000 less than the S2 Cabriolet), while the evergreen 944 Turbo (complete with a new rear spoiler) was DM 97,175.

In the UK, the S2 coupé was priced at £32,024 (about £4700 less than the S2 Cabriolet), and the Turbo was listed at £39,893. *What Car?* tried the soft-top model, and concluded: "Judged in its own right, the S2 Cabriolet is a very special car. But when you think

*Below and following two pages: Various views of the 1990 S2 Cabriolet for the home market. During a test of the S2 Cabriolet,* Road & Track *observed: "In top-down driving, wind flow is well managed in the 944. The top of the windshield is close enough to the driver's head to make a good pocket of calm air in the cockpit, with a small but liveable amount of buffeting around the top of the head."*

*The 1990 S2 Cabriolet for the home market.*

help wishing for a crack in the facade just to prove that the machine is, so to speak, human."

## American update

For the 1990 model year (introduced in October '89), both S2 models were fitted with dual airbags, but the standard

*A UK-registered S2 Cabriolet pictured at the MIRA testing facility. (Courtesy MIRA)*

how much it costs over the fixed-head 944, it's rather less appealing. It has a much poorer low-speed ride, isn't quite as quick (though the difference is all but academic) and lacks an element of practicality in that it's even less of a 2+2." Obviously, the shine was starting to wear off.

Meanwhile, after time with the S2 coupé, *MotorSport* stated: "It is odd to be able to reconcile the sensational performance of a car like the 944 S2 with its everyday placidity, but if you can live with the shallow boot, restricted ventilation and that awful handbrake position, and have mastered the hit-and-miss switch layout across the striking dash, then (assuming your company is paying the purchase price), you will be hard put to find any imbalance, let alone weakness, in its spread of ability ... somehow, the four-cylinder Porsches are so universally competent that it's almost disappointing. Like the school swot who excels in all fields, one can't

*Interior of the American spec S2 coupé, with a traditional 924/944 rear seat and luggage cover. Note the four-spoke steering wheel design introduced for the driver's-side airbag.*

departure of Peter Schutz. Branitzski, who had been with Porsche since 1965, wanted to retire, but after Ferry Porsche asked him to stay on, he agreed to continue until a suitable replacement could be found. Having done a sterling job in a difficult situation, in March 1990 Branitzski finally managed to hand over the reins to Arno Bohn, a

944 was dropped and the Turbo was only available to special order. Prices remained the same as those quoted for the previous season. This was probably because just 9479 cars had been sold in the States during 1989 - a pitiful number compared with that posted a few years earlier. Heinz Branitzski said at the time: "This is undoubtedly the most difficult year we have ever had in America. Hopefully, the worst is behind us." But it wasn't; sales for the 1990 calendar year dropped by another 340 units. Given that the 2.7 litre 944 had gone, and the imminent end of the Turbo, I suppose it could have been a lot worse.

## Branitzski makes his exit

Heinz Branitzski was made the Stuttgart company's Chairman after the

*Rear seats of the same 1990 S2 coupé, complete with the newly-introduced three-point seatbelts.*

young high-flyer who'd made his name in the computer world.

Rumours circulating during the final months of 1990 suggested the possibility of a six-speed manual gearbox for the 944. As it happened, the prediction was a good one: although the 944 never did get this transmission, its replacement did.

## The Turbo Cabriolet

The 944 Turbo Cabriolet was announced with the other 1991 cars in August 1990. Available from February, it was to be built in strictly limited numbers, combining the 250bhp turbocharged engine with the S2 Cabriolet body. Weighing only 22lbs (10kg) more than the S2 version, its performance was naturally fantastic, with a top speed of 162mph. A truly stunning machine.

After testing the vehicle, *MotorSport* noted in the July 1991 issue: "The 944 Turbo Cabriolet offers a rapid and honest sports car, but one without the traditional drawbacks. The ride is firm without inflicting jarring shocks on the occupants, but the harder you drive, the more sense it makes.

"The 944 Turbo Cabriolet is a limited edition that may well be worth collecting. It was certainly one of our better motoring experiences of 1991."

*Fast Lane* compared the same car with a Maserati Spyder. With the Maserati costing substantially less but with the same power output (the Italian thoroughbred had more torque), it was a worthy competitor. However, the Porsche had the better sorted chassis, and it was this that tipped the balance in favour of the Stuttgart machine.

*The highly-desirable 944 Turbo Cabriolet. Announced in August 1990, by the time it was discontinued, 625 examples had been made, 100 of which found their way onto the UK market.*

*Right: Although already killed off in America, the 944 Turbo continued to be sold in Europe alongside S2 models for the 1991 season. By the time production came to an end, a total of 25,348 turbocharged 944s had been built.*

*Right, inset: Interior of the home market S2 coupé with dual airbags and a split rear seat.*

From my experience, although very demanding, the beautifully-appointed Maserati had a wonderful character; troublesome, but still wonderful. Even as a Porsche fan (although my loyalty for the Italian marque can be measured in equal terms), on a value for money basis, it would have definitely got my vote.

Although a figure of 500 Turbo Cabriolets was mentioned at first, ultimately, 625 were built. Of this total, 100 were right-hand drive models for the UK market, priced at £46,993 each. The last cars were eventually sold in mid-1992.

## Other 1991 model year news

With the end of the 944 in sight, there were few changes for 1991. The turbocharged car continued as it was, while the S2 models gained some minor gearbox modifications (all internal ratios and the final-drive were carried over), an internal adjustment switch for the headlights and an integrated central locking/alarm system as standard. In addition, the S2 coupé received the new rear spoiler introduced on the 1990 Turbo. The 944 Turbo left the American arena once and for all in July 1990, but the S2 models soldiered on for a bit longer. Price lists for 1991 quoted $44,050 for the coupé, and $51,050 for the drophead. In Britain, the S2 coupé was listed at £35,682, and the Cabriolet

> **Standard coachwork colours (1991 MY)**
> Black, Maritime Blue, Guards Red, Azure Blue, Alpine White, Rubystone Red.
>
> **Special coachwork colours**
> Crystal Silver Metallic, Cyclamen Red Metallic, Cobalt Blue Metallic, Titanium Metallic, Glacier Blue Metallic, Panther Black Metallic.
>
> **Trim materials**
> Black, blue or grey leatherette with matching inlays. Alternatively, seat facings could also be supplied in black, blue or grey 'Porsche' cloth, Studio Check cloth or leather as an option. Carpets came in black, blue or grey. The Cabriolet hood was available in black, blue or grey.

commanded a further £5222; the Turbo, which continued in European markets, was priced at £42,718. Out of interest, the UK 911 range started at £47,198 at this time. However, in the April budget, VAT went up from 15% to 17.5%, so that the cheapest 944 was now £36,458.

Despite the high price, *Autocar &*

*The 1991 model year S2 coupé featured the same rear spoiler as that introduced on the Turbo the previous season.*

*An early 1991 model year S2 Cabriolet fascia (all post-February 1991 left-hand drive cars came with dual airbags as standard).*

*From this angle, the 944 S2 Cabriolet looked absolutely stunning. Sadly, like the rest of the 944 models, the 1991 model year was its last sales season, although a number of unsold cars later found buyers who preferred the older 944 shape to that of the new 968.*

*Left, top: A beautiful publicity shot of the 1991 Cabriolet. Sadly, this model came to represent the end of an era, as, for the 1992 season, there was a new four-cylinder car - the 968.*

*Left, bottom: The 968 was undoubtedly a quick machine, the six-speed model covering 0-60 in 6.3 seconds before going on to a top speed of 156mph (250kph), and came in both coupé and convertible guise.*

*Motor* still felt that the S2 coupé was the best GT car available on the UK market. It said: "Shortlisted were such stars as the beautifully-engineered Audi Quattro, the fast and effective Nissan 200SX, the highly-desirable Renault-Alpine GTA Turbo, the crisp and efficient VW Corrado G60 and the stunningly different Alfa SZ Coupé. That the 944 wards off these challenges to come out ahead only adds to its considerable esteem. It also underlines just how effective a continuous research and development programme can be, and how such a philosophy can triumph over much more recent designs."

Having decided to move four-cylinder production from Neckarsulm to Stuttgart, the 944 line started rolling in March 1991 in preparation for the forthcoming 968 to be built there. After all, with falling sales figures, the Zuffenhausen plant could now provide more than enough capacity, rendering the need to pay for the Neckarsulm facility unnecessary. By now, airbags had become standard on all left-hand drive models, incidentally.

Ultimately, less than 600 S2s were constructed at Werk V in Zuffenhausen when the series was killed off (no turbocharged 944s were built after the move to Porsche's home town). By the time the end of the road arrived in July 1991, the S2 coupé was priced at DM 84,555 and the Cabriolet was a massive DM 95,760.

Total 944 S2 coupé production added up to 11,471 units, of which, just over 2000 went to the States, while 6059 S2 Cabriolets were built

*Another view of the two 968 models available at the time of the launch, officially held at the 1991 Frankfurt Show (the 968 finally reached the UK market in the spring of 1992). The Cabriolet had an electrically-operated hood, incidentally.*

(2386 of these ended up in America). The 944 Turbo was discontinued in the same month. Including the Turbo Cup cars and the limited edition convertible model, a total of 25,348 turbocharged 944s were built - twice as many as the 924 Turbo production run if the pure racers and Carrera GTs are discounted.

## Another F1 project

Surprisingly, given its poor performance in the American CART series (at least by the standards expected from Porsche), after an approach from Footwork, in February 1990, the Stuttgart company once again returned to the F1 arena. This time, however, the situation was a little riskier as the 3.5 litre V12 cam-covers proudly carried Porsche insignia, putting the Zuffenhausen concern firmly in the spotlight, and the Footwork Arrows chassis it was destined to be installed in was certainly a lot less competitive than that of the McLaren.

Max Welti, former Sauber Mercedes Group C Team Manager, was appointed head of the F1 programme at Weissach. His brief was to ensure that the Milton Keynes-based Footwork team had at least ten engines available for each race in the 1991 season.

Early testing was marred by a series of problems, and, sadly, things didn't improve on the track. Early hopes for 700bhp at 14,000rpm by the end of the first season were dashed (official figures quoted 650bhp at 12,000rpm), and the unit was found to be far too heavy to be competitive. This was a very disappointing chapter in Porsche history - the only finishes recorded during 1991 were when the Footwork chassis was fitted with a Cosworth engine, and even then no points were scored. In the end, the joint project was formally abandoned on the eve of the Japanese Grand Prix. The Footwork equipe signed up with Mugen-Honda for 1992.

## US review

For the German company, 1991 had been a disaster as far as sales were concerned. Only 4400 Porsches found

*This cutaway of the 968 - the replacement for the 944 - clearly shows the model's heritage.*

new homes, with the 911 accounting for almost three-quarters of this total. Frederick J. Schwab, PCNA's new President, certainly had a tough battle on his hands.

The last few 944s were sold off in the States during the early part of 1992 (in a bid to sell the final batch of coupés, Britain introduced the 'SE' version with an uprated engine and suspension, incidentally), but even the arrival of the 968 could do nothing to halt the downward spiral of US sales figures. It would be 1994 before they started to pick up again, thanks purely to the success of the new 911.

At least, if nothing else, the 944 was beginning to prove its worth on American race tracks, where the S2 models dominated the Grand Sports category of the Firehawk endurance series. This generated a good deal of publicity, of course, but failed to secure more sales. Fortunately for Schwab, introduction of the Boxster for the 1997 season boosted marque popularity. Nearly 7000 examples of the new roadster were sold during its first year on the US market.

## End of the line - the 968

Prototype pictures of the 968 started to appear in magazines during mid-1991. It looked very similar to the 944, but disguise panels around the headlights and tail kept the final details out of reach of the long lens brigade until the car was launched at that year's Frankfurt Show.

Mechanically similar to the 944 S2, it was powered by a development of the S2 unit, and linked to either a

*American advertising from 1992.*

Getrag six-speed manual or four-speed Tiptronic semi-automatic gearbox. The three-litre, four-cylinder, dohc 16v engine featured VarioCam (Porsche's variable inlet valve timing system), pushing power output up to 240bhp at 6200rpm and maximum torque to 225lbft at 4100rpm; in line with Porsche's 'world engine' policy, US models developed a near-identical 236bhp.

Like the 944, the 968 was available in both closed coupé and Cabriolet guise. The body styling, executed by Harm Laagay (the man credited with the lines for the 924, and now head of Porsche's styling department following the retirement of Tony Lapine), was a cross between the 944 and 928, although 80% of the panelwork was new. Perhaps not surprisingly, however, in order to keep costs down, the interior was basically very similar to that of the 944 it replaced.

In early 1992 rumours of a cheaper convertible and coupé - supposedly priced significantly lower than the 968 - surfaced again. Some even suggested a link between the drophead model and Mercedes-Benz, a suggestion quickly dismissed as rubbish by the venerable Paul Frere, who had a closer relationship with staff at the Zuffenhausen factory than most.

The Boxster arrived in late-1996 (for the 1997 model year), but a price tag of $40,000 meant it could hardly be classed as cheap. At that time, a closed version was not planned. Frere's comments were proved correct as the months passed; not surprising, really, given that the management wanted Porsche to remain a specialist rather than volume producer.

Meanwhile, in the face of falling sales, the 968 Club Sport was introduced for the 1993 season. Whilst retaining the standard 240bhp engine, it sported the optional 17-inch wheels and tyres, and was both substantially lighter and cheaper (£28,975 in the UK) due to a fairly basic specification. The 968 CS duly won the *Autocar*'s inaugural 'Car of the Year' award, while *MotorSport* said: "From start to finish, we loved it. It's a pure driving delight."

1993 also saw the birth of the 968 Turbo S, powered by a 305bhp version of the three-litre engine. Being 110lbs (50kg) lighter than even the CS, it was

*The Porsche marque still carried three basic lines, as this picture, taken for the 1995 model year, shows (from left to right): the 928, 911 and 968. However, both the 928 and 968 were discontinued before the 1996 range was announced.*

capable of over 165mph and a sub-five second 0-60 time. Very few were built, though rarer still was the 968 Turbo RS - a lightweight customer racing version with 337bhp and 367lbft of torque on tap. One raced at Le Mans in 1994, but, sadly, crashed out of the French classic.

In January 1994, the UK received its own unique model known as the Sport; basically, a CS with a few added luxuries. Like the Club Sport, it was available as a coupé only, and, like its predecessor, it also appealed to the press. Simon Arron wrote: "No frills. No unnecessary electronic gizmos. Just straightforward driving pleasure. Amen for that."

For 1995, the Club Sport was priced at £29,975, with the Sport another £3020 on top of that. The standard 968 coupé was £37,495 (or £39,750 with the Tiptronic transmission), while the Cabriolet came in at £40,695. Again, the semi-automatic version was just over £2000 more. However, this was the last year that a 968 could be bought - it failed to appear in the 1996 brochures. In the *Autocar*, Andrew Frankel stated that "the 968 had become, in Club Sport guise, the finest handling car that even mildly unreasonable money could buy; a hedonistic cocktail of electrifying throttle response, the finest power steering in the world and the kind of on-limit behaviour that proved there was a heaven after all."

Ironically, the flawless and utterly forgiving character of the 968 may have been its undoing, as traditional Porsche buyers were looking for something a little more demanding, something that would provide a little more excitement. By coincidence, the end of the 928 series came at the same time, leaving only the evergreen 911 in the Porsche line-up until the Boxster made its debut. Considering that the 928 was supposed to replace the 911 range some 15 years earlier, this can only be regarded as yet another irony.

A total of 12,793 968s were made between introduction in 1991 and the end of production during the summer of 1995, 4389 of which were Cabriolets. Just under 4000 went to the States, split roughly 50/50 between coupés and soft-top models.

## APPENDIX I
BUYING AND RESTORATION

The 944 series has always been loved by press and owners alike. This, combined with a reputation for solidity, reliability and a minimal thirst for fuel, has meant that most are snapped up the minute they reach the second-hand market. Consequently, residual values have remained high.

There is nothing wrong with this - indeed, it's a sure sign of a high-quality machine - but it does bring with it the potential for an unscrupulous seller to try and turn a high profit on the back of the unwary. Be certain that what you are buying is worth the money, and not a rough example made to look good for a quick sale.

The advice, as always, is buy the best example you can afford, as it will save money in the long run. Join a Porsche Club, and enlist its help to ensure that the car is good value before you part with any cash. Spending out on club membership is an investment that will pay dividends, giving you the chance to speak to fellow owners who've had similar problems, providing a route to cheaper spares, and a must nowadays for a lot of agreed value, classic car insurance policies. Below are a few thoughts and some brief pointers on what to look for when buying a 944:

### Body
From the word go, the 944 came with an extensive seven year bodywork warranty, extended to ten years after 1986. Porsche could afford to do this because it had invested a great deal of time, energy and money in the car before launch, rather than trying to rectify a problem later.

Although a few 944s have suffered from rust, most well looked after examples should still be in pristine condition. The main reason for this is that Porsche applied a zinc coat at 500 degrees C to galvanise the body, inside and out, and a good coating of underseal. Nevertheless, still check for any sign of rust.

Look for evidence of crash damage (the engine and transmission mounts can give a good indication of whether a car has been involved in an accident) and, if panels have been replaced, are they the proper galvanised items or cheaper substitutes? Panel gaps are another good clue - some are ridiculously wide by today's standards, but they should always be uniform. Different shades of paint and overspray is further evidence of repair work.

The nose is very susceptible to stone chips, and water has been known to leak into the passenger compartment through the sunroof. This isn't a particularly serious problem, but remember that Porsche carpets and/or headlinings are not cheap to replace. Also, if left unattended for too long, it could eventually result in a rusty floorpan.

### Exterior trim
Exterior trim, what little there is of it, is generally of a very high quality, but expensive to replace. Light lenses can be costly because so many 944s have survived: second-hand driving light covers are like gold dust, apparently. These are very prone to stone damage

*Cutaway drawing of the 944. This picture appeared in a preliminary catalogue for the model at the time of its launch.*

and cost a fortune to buy through official channels.

A 1984 survey suggested that electrical maladies (including faults with the windscreen wipers) were a source of aggravation, although compared to British and Italian cars from this period, it's hardly a significant problem, though worth bearing in mind.

Door handles have been known to jam, and remember to use two hands when closing the glass hatch, as abuse will result in the locating pins wearing which will prevent the panel from seating properly. Water (and noise) can then enter the passenger compartment.

### Engine

Obviously, do all of the usual checks for a second-hand car, like looking for leaks, a smoky exhaust, signs of head gasket failure (particularly important on a 944 with its all-alloy construction, though oil in the water could be from the intercooler on earlier turbocharged models), checking compression, oil pressure, and so on. The engine should run exceptionally smoothly, regardless of mileage - if it doesn't, walk away. Whatever it is that's making the unit appear lumpy, it is almost certainly going to be costly to put right.

The 944 had a 12,000 mile service interval when it was new (although it should be noted that a quick check-over and oil and filter change was recommended every 6000 miles). However, going beyond the specified limit is certainly not recommended. Indeed, fresh oil is a must if the engine is to last as long as it should, and the belts that drive the balance shafts need regular checks to avoid expensive consequences. A service record is crucial here, as special tools are needed to do the latter job properly on pre-

185

*This overhead shot of the 1985 Turbo engine, transaxle and running gear also shows the suspension layout, which was basically similar on all 944 series models.*

1987 cars. This is doubly important for the 944 Turbo which, although not as fragile as the 924 Turbo, can still be relatively expensive to maintain. With the Turbo, a service record is an absolute must, and care should be taken not to push the engine when cold and to let it idle for a while before shutting down. Like all Porsche units, if you look after the engine, treating it with a dash of mechanical sympathy if it has a high mileage, it will look after you.

Exhaust systems should last for between two and three years. Replacing a complete 944 system on an early car is cheap enough, but some exhaust components, particularly those relating to emissions equipment (such as catalytic converters), can be fiercely expensive. If it's intended to keep the car for any length of time, it's probably worth investing in a stainless steel exhaust with a lifetime guarantee.

For those mechanically-challenged individuals who want to buy a car, the best advice on offer is to consult an independent specialist or a local Porsche Club representative. The engine is an expensive component to put right, and a *Motor Trend* survey conducted in 1984 revealed that almost half of the early 944s had suffered some kind of mechanical trouble, with engine mounting failure the most common complaint. This was subsequently rectified, but it just goes to show that even one of Germany's most prestigious marques is not immune to problems.

Take heart, though, from the fact that when asked if they would buy another 944, 92% of owners interviewed said that they would. Furthermore, based on their experience of the 944, over 96% of them said that they would happily stay with the Stuttgart marque: perhaps the fact that three-quarters of the owners rated overall quality and workmanship as 'excellent' had something to do with it.

## Transmission

Porsche gearboxes are fairly robust, so gearchange quality should be very good. Vibration in the propshaft could be very expensive to repair, and although a clutch is quite cheap to buy, the time needed to fit it can lead to a nasty bill. Clutches seem to last for around 50,000 miles on normally-aspirated cars, and something like 30,000 miles on Turbos. Look for leaks on earlier automatic gearboxes and, naturally, there should not be any leaks from the transaxle unit.

## Suspension, steering & braking system

Front wheel shimmy is a recognised problem in high mileage 944s - tyres are often at fault, so check for even wear across the tread. This will also give an indication of the condition and/or alignment of suspension and steering components.

The rack should be carefully checked for play (and leaks, as repair kits are not available), and the power steering fluid reservoir had a reputation for leaking before an improved clip was fitted. The brake calipers have been known to seize on cars that haven't had service schedules kept up-to-date; the bill for brake pads, especially those for the Turbo, are not for the faint-hearted. ABS is a bonus, but only on a well-maintained example.

For those trying to run the car on a budget, many parts can be sourced from cheaper outlets, but components under this heading have a distinct bearing on safety, so avoid anything a mechanic wouldn't put on his own vehicle. Naturally, if it comes from a Porsche dealer, it's guaranteed to do the job properly, but will be much more expensive. Exercise a little common sense and caution - there is rarely such a thing as a true bargain!

Most of the tyres employed by the 944 range are freely available and can be bought quite cheaply, if you shop around. As well as making sure they are the right size, ensure they are of the correct rating also.

Wheels are another matter, of course, so should be in good condition. However, there's no shortage of second-hand Porsche spares dealers if money is tight. Wheels should be cleaned regularly, by the way, to avoid deterioration caused by brake dust.

*Cutaway of the 1989 944 Turbo. Comparing this drawing to that of the earlier normally-aspirated car highlights a number of important differences under the skin, though the flavour of the original was still very much in evidence.*

### Interior

Seats wear exceptionally well, but often split at the seams (the optional leather trim is a big selling point, incidentally). The 924-style dashboards often crack due to drying out by the sun, and steering wheels have been known to do the same on occasion. Replacement is the only obvious, though expensive, answer, although in many cases it may be possible to find a good second-hand one.

### Spares today

The German requirement that spare parts be manufactured for ten years after the end of a model's production run has ensured that most mechanical components are still available. Almost everything, except for the odd bits of trim, can be sourced at very reasonable cost, and, if prepared to pay the price, it's fair to say that there isn't anything of note that cannot be bought at a Porsche dealership.

### The best buy?

To quote Quentin Wilson, the well-known British journalist and car dealer: "Ask me which second-hand sports car makes the best buy and I'll reel off three numbers - 944. I've bought and sold enough of them to know that it's probably one of the most underrated performance cars around. From a dealer's point of view, sell a used 944 and the only time you'll ever see the man again is when he comes back for another. The car makes so much sense: low depreciation, cheap to buy, reasonable maintainance, lots of image, an unimpeachable bloodline and that sparkling performance. And remember, it isn't Japanese.

"The 944 is one of the most economical and reliable 140mph sports cars I know of. Compared to Ferrari 308s and XJSs, 944s are for nothing. In short, Porsche's most successful product is a sensible sports car - a contradiction in terms if ever there was one - but not a description you can apply to many other cars of this ilk."

The standard 944 has a relatively modest amount of power compared to some of the later additions to the range, but the chassis is absolutely delightful. However, good examples, especially those built after 1985, hold their price well, and there are many other vehicles that can provide the same level of performance and handling much more cheaply. Of course, a Porsche is a Porsche, and for enthusiasts of the marque, nothing else can provide that special feeling when you slip behind the wheel.

If going down this route, remember that the 924S, with its lithe body and similar engine, also has a lot to offer. The Turbo has great performance, but, to go with its exotic turn of speed, there are exotic maintenance bills. This model should not be regarded as a "poor man's Porsche" - given what it costs, make sure it's the car you want, as long-term running costs can be much the same as for a normally-aspirated 911.

The 16v models are a good compromise between the early 2.5 litre models and the Turbo, the larger displacement S2s offering excellent performance throughout the rev range, and Turbo-style bodies without turbo lag. Being newer, and possibly the most desirable, expect to pay out a lot initially and budget sensibly for the future. The soft-top versions, of course, offer a very special experience, but are thin on the ground.

All 944 models have different characters, and prices vary wildly depending on which it is and where you look. Find the right car to suit your needs (for instance, will you use it every day or just at weekends?), your personality and your wallet, and have it checked over by someone familiar with the series. The fact that a 944 is still as good to drive today as it was a couple of decades ago makes it a very attractive proposition. Low depreciation, the chance of classic, low mileage insurance, and surprisingly good fuel economy are added bonuses.

## APPENDIX II
### PRODUCTION DETAILS

For production vehicles, the model years are used for dates, whereas competition models and specials are shown with calendar years. The chassis numbers shown are the first in each batch which, in almost all cases, ran consecutively thereafter.

### 944

| MY | Prod. | Notes | Chassis No. |
|---|---|---|---|
| 1982 | 3921 | Europe/RoW | ZZZ94ZCN400001 |
| 1983 | 24,633 | Europe/RoW | ZZZ94ZDN400001 |
|  |  | US/Canada/Japan | AA094-DN450001 |
| 1984 | 26,539 | Europe/RoW | ZZZ94ZEN400001 |
|  |  | US/Canada/Japan | AA094-EN450001 |
| 1985 | 14,029 | Europe/RoW | ZZZ94ZFN400001 |
|  |  | US/Canada/Japan | AA094-FN450001 |
| 1985.5 | 9691 | Europe/RoW | ZZZ94ZFN420001 |
|  |  | US/Canada | AA094-FN470001 |
| 1986 | 17,010 | Europe/RoW | ZZZ94ZGN400001 |
|  |  | US/Canada | AA094-GN450001 |
| 1987 | 10,589 | Europe/RoW | ZZZ94ZHN420001 |
|  |  | US/Canada | AA094-HN470001 |
| 1988 | 5957 | Europe/RoW | ZZZ94ZJN420001 |
|  |  | US/Canada | AA094-JN470001 |
| 1989 | 5421 | Europe/RoW | ZZZ94ZKN400001 |
|  |  | US/Canada | AA094-KN450001 |

### 944 Turbo

| MY | Prod. | Notes | Chassis No. |
|---|---|---|---|
| 1985.5 | 283 | Europe/RoW | ZZZ95ZFN100001 |
|  |  | US/Canada | AA095-FN150001 |
| 1986 | 10,937 | Europe/RoW | ZZZ95ZGN100001 |
|  |  | Europe/RoW | ZZZ95ZGN140001 |
|  |  | US/Canada | AA095-GN150001 |
| 1987 | 4974 | Europe/RoW | ZZZ95ZHN100001 |
|  |  | US | AA295-HN150001 |
|  |  | Canada | AA295OHN160001 |
| 1988 | 3875* | Europe/RoW | ZZZ95ZJN100001 |
|  |  | US | AA295-JN150001 |
|  |  | Canada | AA295OJN160001 |
| 1989 | 2693 | Europe/RoW | ZZZ95ZKN100001 |

*Figure includes Turbo S and SE.

Frere, Paul 31, 52, 66, 182
Freund, Jochen 26, 41, 159
Frock, Rainer 138
Fuhrmann, Dr Ernst 9, 17, 20, 25-26, 29-31, 34, 40-41

Geneva Show 8, 29, 45, 48, 67
Ghia 17
Giugiaro, Giorgetto 24
GM 27
Goetze 17
Gorissen, Wolfhelm 138
Griffin, Larry 77, 120
Gugelot 18
Gulf 21
Gurney, Dan 12

Harris, F.L.M. 67
Hensler, Paul 26, 30, 41, 88
Herrarte Ariano, J. 11
Herrmann, Hans 22
Hill, Phil 104
Hitler, Adolf 6
Hockenheim 114
Hoffman, Max 8-9, 12
Holbert, Al 34, 141
Honda 77, 179

Ickx, Jacky 37
IMSA 22, 139, 181
Int. GT Trophy 22

Jaguar 11, 29, 78, 96, 104, 132, 158, 187
Japanese GP 179
Jarama 114
Jeep 54

Kacher, George 57
Karmann 18, 24-25
Kirchdorfer, Gerhard 41
Knoop, Rick 76, 88
Kohl, Dr Helmut 67
Komenda, Erwin 8, 15

Lagaay, Harm 27, 182
Lake, Barry 57
Lamborghini 96, 135
Lanchester, Dr F.W. 44
Lapine, Tony 27, 88, 138, 166, 182
Larrouse, Gerard 22
Leiding, Rudolf 22, 24
Le Mans 12, 22, 32, 34, 36-38, 41, 44, 52, 63, 88, 101, 114, 140, 143, 183
Liège-Rome-Liège 9, 11
Linge, Herbert 9, 16
Lohner 5
Lotus 12, 28, 59, 78, 121
Lotz, Kurt 18-19, 22

Marathon de la Route 22
Marchart, Horst 138

Marko, Helmut 22
Maserati 127, 158, 174
Mazda 28, 31, 60, 63, 76, 103-104, 106, 127
McLaren 77, 179
Mezger, Hans 77
Mille Miglia 11-12, 104
MIRA 172
Mitchell, Bill 27
Mitsubishi 44, 54, 60, 107-108, 127
Monte Carlo Rally 15-16, 22
Monza 114
Moss, Stirling 12
*Motor* 59, 98, 120
*MotorSport* 59, 67, 96, 120, 136, 158, 172, 174, 182
*Motor Trend* 34, 65, 88, 168, 186
Mugen 179
Muller, Herbert 22

NEC (British) Motor Show 157
Nelson Ledges 76, 88
Nichols, Mel 34
Nordhoff, Heinz 8, 17-18, 25
NSU 19, 22, 27, 30, 52
Nürburgring 9, 12, 22

Opel 22, 27

Palmer, Brian 77
Paris Salon 8-9, 23, 29
*Performance Car* 106, 144, 159
Peugeot 15, 41
Piech, Anton 6
Piech, Ferdinand 16-17, 19-20, 127
Piech, Louise 16, 20
Polensky, Helmut 9
Pontiac 76
*Popular Classics* 57
Porsche, Butzi 14-15, 20, 27
Porsche, Ferdinand 5-6, 8
Porsche, Ferry 5-6, 8, 12, 14-16, 18, 20, 24, 37, 40, 127, 173
Porsche+Audi 19, 23, 87
Porsche Cars GB 67, 73, 96-97, 109, 157
Porsche Cars N.America 87, 118, 129, 141, 181
Porsche Design 20
Prost, Alain 77
Pucci, Antonio 16

Rabe, Karl 8
RAC Rally 22
Renault (-Alpine) 6, 41, 121, 179
Reutter 8
*Road & Track* 27, 30, 41, 52, 65-67, 76-77, 103-104, 106, 114, 122, 140, 154, 157, 169
Road Atlanta 143
*Road Test* 23
Rohrl, Walter 35, 37
Rolls-Royce 67
Rondeau 38
Rouse, Andy 34, 38

Ruhrl, Rudolf 7

Saab 60
Salzburgring 114, 125
Sauber 179
SCCA 22, 32, 76, 139, 141, 143
Schmid, D. 22
Schmidt, Helmut 23, 67
Schmucher, Toni 24
Schurti, Manfred 34, 38
Schutz, Peter 40, 54, 57, 67, 96, 125, 127, 173
Schwab, F.J. 181
Sebring 12, 16
Seidel, Wolfgang 12
Sloniger, Jerry 57
Sonauto 114
Spa 114
St Antoine, Arthur 118
Steyr 5
Strosek 99
Stuck, Hans 7

TAG 77, 154
Targa Florio 11-12, 16-17, 22
Tomala, Hans 15
Tour de France Auto. 12
Tourist Trophy 12
Toyota 60, 127, 158-159
Turbo Cup Series 111-114, 124-125, 135, 141, 143, 179
TVR 59

Van Lennep, Gijs 22
Volkswagen 5-6, 8-9, 17-20, 22-27, 31, 41, 67, 87, 111, 125, 179
Volvo 41
Von Neumann, John 9
Von Senger, R. 6
VW-Porsche VG 18-20, 24-25, 141

Waldegaard, Bjorn 22
Walker, Rob 12
Welti, Max 179
Wendler 12
*What Car?* 101, 121, 168
Williams 77
Willow Springs 77, 122
Wilson, Quentin 187
Winkelhock, Joachim 111
World Rally Champs. 35, 37
Wyer, John 21

Zagato 12
Zasada, S. 15
Zeltweg 22

*The Porsche company and its products are are mentioned throughout the book.*

# INDEX

Abarth 12
Abarth, Carlo 6
AC 59
AFN 10
Alfa Romeo 12, 27-28, 31, 59-60, 104, 153, 179
*Alternative Cars* 59
Alvis 67
AMC 26
Andersson, Ake 22
Arron, Simon 183
Arrows 179
ASC 161-162, 168
Attwood, Richard 22
Audi 19-20, 22-23, 25-27, 30-31, 37, 41, 46, 54, 59, 109, 127, 179
Austro-Daimler 5
*Autocar (& Motor)* 57, 59-60, 98, 101, 136, 153, 159, 176, 182-183
*Auto Motor und Sport* 31
Auto Union 6
*Auto Zeitung* 71

Baker, Freddy 76, 88, 143
Ballot-Lena, Claude 22
Balzarini, G. 16
Barth, Edgar 12
Barth, Jurgen 34, 37
Baur 161, 166
Bell, Derek 34, 37
Bell, Roger 58, 133
Berlin-Rome Race 6
Bez, Dr Ulrich 138
BMW 60, 96, 129, 132, 138, 161
Boddy, William 67
Bohn, Arno 174
Bolster, John 31
Bond, James 59
Borgward 12
Bott, Helmuth 26, 41, 44, 47, 54, 138
Bowler, Brian 129
Branitzki, Heinz 20, 57, 125, 127, 144, 154, 173
Brunn (Brno) 114
Bulbeck, Peter 157
Bundy, Doc 63
Busby, Jim 63, 76, 88

Cadillac 106
Can-Am 23
*Car & Driver* 77, 88, 118, 121, 127, 136
Carlsen Racing 143
Carl Zeiss 125

Carrera Panamericana 11-12
*Cars Are My Life* 24
CART 179
Ceppos, Rich 127
Chasseuil, Guy 22
Chevrolet 67, 70, 76-77, 103-104, 143
Cisitalia 6
*Classic Cars* 58, 77, 101
Connaught 10
Cook, John 129
Cosworth 121, 179
Csere, Csaba 121
CSI 12

Daimler (Germany) 5
Daimler-Benz (Mercedes) 5-6, 19, 29, 54, 60, 96, 158, 179, 182
Datsun (Nissan) 27-28, 31, 60, 76-77, 104, 121, 127, 179
Davis, Colin 16
Daytona 22
De Lorean 41, 57
DeTomaso 158
Deutz 40
Dinkel, John 30, 114
Dodge 76
Drauz 11
Dron, Tony 34, 101
Dusio, Piero 6

Earls Court Show 10, 19, 29, 57
Eickwinkel, Uwe 114
Eifelrennen 12
Elford, Vic 15
European Grand Prix 6

*Fast Lane* 108, 153, 174
Ferrari 67, 70, 96, 135, 187
FIA 12, 34
Finch, David 143
Floridia, P. 22
Footwork 179
Ford 17, 24, 58-60, 76, 121
Formula One (GP) 6, 12, 26, 77, 104, 154, 179
Formula Two 12
*For Your Eyes Only* 59
Frankel, Andrew 183
Frankfurt Show 11, 14-16, 19, 27, 31-32, 52, 73, 104, 109, 115, 118, 179, 181
Frazer-Nash 10
French Grand Prix 12

| MY | Prod. | Notes | Chassis No. |
|---|---|---|---|
| | | US/Canada | AA295-KN150001 |
| 1990 | 1233 | Europe/RoW | ZZZ95ZLN100001 |
| | | US/Canada | AA295-LN150001 |
| 1991 | 411 | Europe/RoW | ZZZ95ZMN100001 |

## 944S

| MY | Prod. | Notes | Chassis No. |
|---|---|---|---|
| 1987 | 5777 | Europe/RoW | ZZZ94ZHN400001 |
| | | US/Canada | AA094-HN450001 |
| 1988 | 7054 | Europe/RoW | ZZZ94ZJN400001 |
| | | US/Canada | AA094-JN450001 |

## 944 Turbo Cup

| MY | Prod. | Notes | Chassis No. |
|---|---|---|---|
| 1987 | 99 | RoW | ZZZ95ZHN104101 |
| | | Canada | AA295OHN165101 |
| 1988 | 193 | RoW | ZZZ95ZJN104001 |
| | | Canada | AA295OJN165001 |
| 1989 | 25 | RoW | ZZZ95ZKN100001 |

## 944 S2

| MY | Prod. | Notes | Chassis No. |
|---|---|---|---|
| 1989 | 4902 | RoW | ZZZ94ZKN402731 |
| | | US/Canada | AB094-KN450001 |
| 1990 | 3321 | RoW | ZZZ94ZLN400001 |
| | | US/Canada | AB094-LN450001 |
| 1991 | 3248 | RoW | ZZZ94ZMN400001 |
| | | US/Canada | AB094-MN410001 |
| | | RoW | ZZZ94ZMS400001 |

## 944 S2 Cabriolet

| MY | Prod. | Notes | Chassis No. |
|---|---|---|---|
| 1990 | 3938 | RoW | ZZZ94ZLN430001 |
| | | US/Canada | CB094-LN480001 |
| 1991 | 2121 | RoW | ZZZ94ZMN430001 |
| | | US/Canada | CB094-MN440001 |
| | | RoW | ZZZ94ZMS430001 |

## 944 Turbo Cabriolet

| MY | Prod. | Notes | Chassis No. |
|---|---|---|---|
| 1991 | 625 | Europe/RoW | ZZZ95ZMN130001 |

Total 944 production .................................................................. 117,790
Total 944 Turbo production ....................................................... 24,406
Total 944S production ................................................................ 12,831
Total 944 Turbo Cup production ..................................................... 317
Total 944 S2 production ............................................................. 11,471
Total 944 S2 Cabriolet production................................................. 6059
Total 944 Turbo Cabriolet production ............................................ 625

**Total series production    173,499 (25,348 of which were turbocharged)**

## Also from Veloce Publishing ...

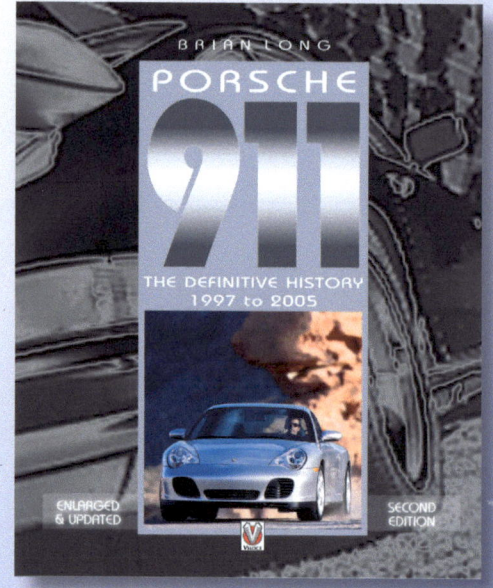

ISBN: 978-1-845848-97-2

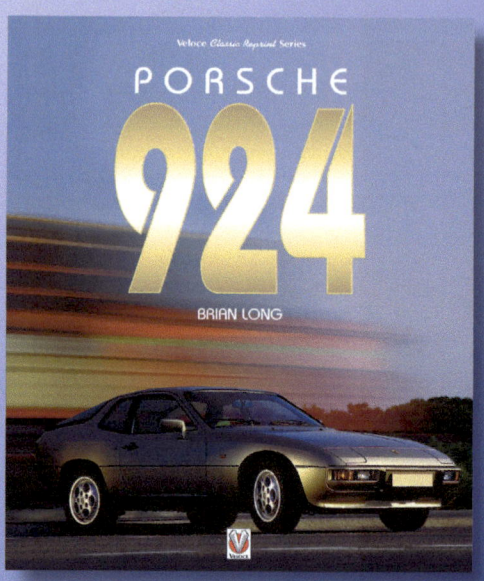

ISBN: 978-1-845849-77-1

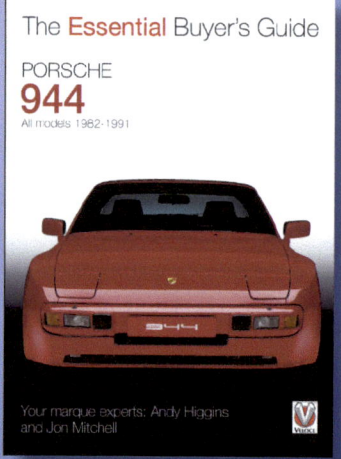

ISBN: 978-1-845845-71-1

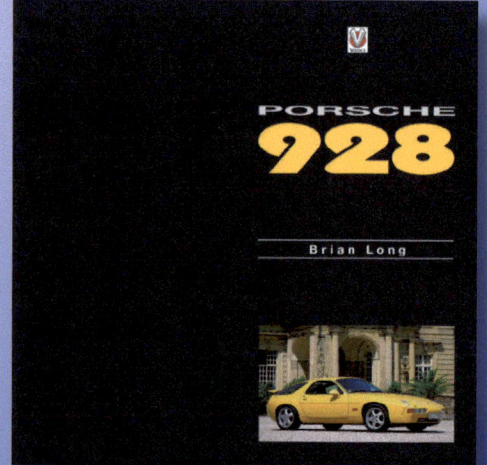

ISBN: 978-1-903706-30-5

ISBN: 978-1-84584-035-8

For more info on Veloce publications see: www.veloce.co.uk
email: info@veloce.co.uk; tel: +44(0) 1305 260068